Proverbs through the Generations

Proverbs through the Generations

Jack Hilliard

K. Mark Hilliard

Jessa Sexton

Franklin, Tennessee

Proverbs through the Generations
Copyright © 2012 by Jack Hilliard, K. Mark Hilliard,
and Jessa Hilliard Sexton
ISBN-13   978-0-9860150-0-7

Edited by Ashley Balding and Jessa Hilliard Sexton
Cover design by Courtney R. Allen
Book Block design by Courtney R. Allen
Illustrations by Courtney R. Allen
Bible references from New King James Version

All rights reserved. No part of this publication may be reproduced or transmitted in any form or by any means without written permission of the author.

Published by Hilliard Press
a division of the
Hilliard Institute for Educational Wellness

edication

It is a great joy to dedicate my part of this book of Proverbs to the life and memory of W. Claude Hall, a great man of God.
—**Jack**

It is a difficult task to dedicate a writing such as this when there are so many people I appreciate. As I thought on this task, I finally decided to dedicate my section of the book to my grandchildren—Charlie, Jack, Jonas, and Isaac—and to my future, yet-to-be grandchildren. While they will not understand this gift today (as they are ages three months through three years old), someday they will be able to read what I have written and hopefully benefit from the words I have passed on. So I dedicate my portion of this book to my future, my grandchildren. I hope you guys discover all my journals and enjoy finding out about the unusual ponderings of Hi-Papa, who loves you very much.

—**Mark**

It is obvious, but I dedicate my portion of writing to my family: the generations before me, my brother, my husband, my sons, and my children to come. Thank you for the lessons I couldn't have learned without your guidance, and thank you for your love through the lessons I couldn't have learned without erring.

My grandparents, those still with me and those I have lost, gave me a solid foundation in love and learning. I hope I make them always proud as I raise one line of their lineage.

Also, I specifically dedicate my writing to my co-writers, Granddaddy Jack and Daddy. People who know me well know my grand fascination of and appreciation for my father: his praises often fill my words. I pray to make him as proud as he has made me feel loved. And for my grandfather, the love and dedication he shows as a husband is the stuff chic flicks are made of, only it is real! If you want to know the meaning of the word "cherish," you should see his beautiful devotion after sixty years of marriage. What a blessing to have this living example always before me.

—**Jessa**

cknowledgement

I would be remise if I did not acknowledge one of my first instructors at Freed Hardeman University. In 1949–1951, Professor W. Claude Hall sparked my interest in many books of the Bible. One in particular that really roused my attention was Proverbs. He made a Biblical classic even more interesting and practical.

Through the years, I have continued to love Solomon's work. At present, I am working on another book of Proverbs to capture the interest and application for my readers, all inspired by this professor and this project.

—Jack

This book happened because of my daughter, Jessa Hilliard Sexton, who is a wonderful lover of words, tradition, and family. What a wonderful idea to have three generations of family—a father, his son, and his granddaughter—read God's word on family relationships and home, as provided by Solomon, and then articulate the personal meaning, each received from these words, in this special book. I love you, Jessa.

I also thank my father and mother, who convinced me to go to college at a time when I would have more readily enjoyed spending those funds on a nice car. Without their dedication to family, and learning, I would not be where I am today. I love you, Mom and Dad.

I thank my son for always being a good son. When you have a son who always, always, strives to do what is right and good, he makes his father look great as well. I love you, Mark-Aaron.

I thank the spouses of my children, because you bring joy and a sense of solid-family to my kiddos. I love you, Jay and Celeste.

And I know I would not be the man I am today without the woman I married over thirty-five years ago. She is the woman God brought to me while I was still a boy of eighteen, and we married at nineteen. I love you, Rosemary.

—Mark

Beyond my family, I am surrounded by a beautiful support system. I thank those of you who encourage me in my pursuit of writing and education. Also, I can never share a writing project without the proofing of my favorite editor, my mother. Thanks for all of the years of catching my split infinitives, typos, and anything else my own weary editing brain couldn't see.

—**Jessa**

Table of Contents

Introduction 13

Chapters by Jack Hilliard

Chapter 1 17

Chapter 2 23

Chapter 3 27

Chapter 4 33

Chapter 5 37

Chapter 6 41

Chapter 7 47

Chapter 8 53

Chapter 9 59

Chapter 10 65

Chapters by K. Mark Hilliard

Chapter 11 71

Chapter 12 77

Chapter 13 83

Chapter 14 91

Chapter 15 99

Chapter 16 105

Chapter 17 113

Chapter 18 121

Chapter 19 127

Chapter 20 133

Chapters by Jessa Hilliard Sexton

Chapter 21 139

Chapter 22 145

Chapter 23 153

Chapter 24 159

Chapter 25 167

Chapter 26 175

Chapter 27 181

Chapter 28 187

Chapter 29 195

Chapter 30 201

Chapter 31 209

About the Authors 215

ntroduction

A Wise Man's Wise Instructions

Jack Hilliard
It was about the middle of June 2011 when one of my sweet granddaughters, Jessa, challenged me to take another look at the astounding book of Proverbs. Her purpose was for me to look at the first ten chapters of that remarkable book to set the pace for a new book she, her dad Mark, and I were to write. I graciously accepted the assignment expecting many rewards for working on this interesting project with her and my son.

By the time I had looked at the first three chapters, I had already received a part of my reward.

I wrote without the comments of commentators for the purpose of being forced to make a deeper personal examination at the text God gave His servant, Solomon. The only time I ever did a personal study of Proverbs was years ago at the request of a dear lady in Bermuda who wanted me to help her look at this work.

Another reason I accepted this challenge was to see what a "regular person" could derive from Solomon's God-given wisdom by reading and contemplating his instructions, advice, and assignments that he gave to all who will read and listen to him.

I profess no scholarly, personal wisdom, and I challenge our readers to read Solomon's great message in the most serious manner possible to see how we can profit by an inspired book written long before any of us entered into God's world. I like to think of our examination as enjoying the sweet perfume of wisdom and understanding that lingers throughout Solomon's record.

K. Mark Hilliard
As someone who at one time was challenged by the idea of actually reading a book and the unfathomable concept of writing a book, I have come to believe that both of these gifts of expression are from God (reading and writing, whether our skills are elementary or academically impressive) and are sacred ways in which we pass a bit of ourselves on to future generations. Like some may choose to collect teacups or wooden ducks, I am a collector of words. I believe I acquired this trait from my father, whom you will never see without a small pad and pen somewhere on his person. I remember church services when he was not preaching—out came the pad and down went his thoughts inspired by something the speaker had shared.

Early on in my personal attempt to take notes, I made the mistake of trying to write down exactly what the speaker had said, and I often found that upon reexamining those phrases they did not speak to me in any comprehensible manner. So I began to capture words, and I set out to translate those words into my way of thinking, and the new words and phrases became my possession, and with possession, understanding came. These words were not simply a possession to be placed on a shelf for viewing, but more of a guardianship or charge to keep and a passion to be released by finding a way to share these words as a new individualized creation—a book. Like musical notes placed together in rhythmic form to create a song, words, when placed together appropriately, create a rhythmic structure of color, shape, sound, and form. Words, well-united, generate smell, taste, and each of the other senses just as strongly as the actual aroma of a cigar or the savory experience of my mother's cheesecake. Why? How? Because of our personal experiences, because of our study of the many symbols we call words, and because of our exposure to a variety of words in a variety of forms—reading other's words.

Proverbs is a poetic arrangement of word-symbols set in a variety of forms to capture its many readers. I find that these thirty-one chapters often repeat the same thoughts and directives, but with the use of different words and different phraseology. If the reader will read all thirty-one chapters, he will connect with some and not with others, but he will connect, because of the multiplicity of word-forms meant to engage each reader.

It has been a pleasure to work with my daughter again on this project—we published a book together after a visiting fellowship at Oxford University a few years back, and we have enjoyed sharing a classroom of students on many occasions. And to be able to read my father's work, my daughter's work, and my own work, all flowing from one generation down through the next, has been a delight. We have left a piece of ourselves behind to share with you. We have attempted to communicate our experiences through our words. And we hope our words can speak to you and your family and that something we share can connect with your experiences, and your life, and you will find meaning in them.

Our words are our paintings, just as Solomon's words are his. While Solomon had the full-hand of God on his words, we pray that at least God's finger in some way guided ours. Some of our thoughts you are sure to like, and others may bring you to question our power of reason, or at least our way of thinking. I encourage you do what we have done, to take the book of Proverbs, and to examine, think, enjoy, and ponder its meaning for you.

I will end this section by sharing something Solomon said in another of his writings, Ecclesiastes 2:24: "There is nothing better for a man than to eat and drink and tell himself that his labor is good." I believe here that God is teaching us a simple lesson. We must eat, we must drink, and we must work. If we can learn to find joy in the simply things of life that we must do every day, we will find what Joseph Campbell called "our bliss." Family life, home life, should lead each of us in finding our bliss, if we can rightly appropriate what God has shared with us through His words. The book of Proverbs provides an enchanting way to discover this bliss.

Jessa Hilliard Sexton

I got the idea for this book years ago, not too long after I typed up my grandfather's handwritten text to his seventh book. I felt a special kind of bond in reading his words, straight from his pen. No one writes anything by hand anymore, it seems, and it may be a dying art—a beautiful sensory experience. Flipping through notebook pages and yellow pad paper, deciphering his scrawling, it was an intimate family moment for me.

I am blessed to come from generations of people who value writing and wisdom. When I think of the Proverbs, I think if the blessing of family, whose purpose is to uplift, motivate, instruct, and love. Because of the support and examples through the generations, I pray my sons find this definition of family to be true in word, and true in our home.

I have read and edited not only my grandfather's work, but my father's writings as well, and I knew that working together on a project was something we had to accomplish. What better topic than the Proverbs, a specific book of instruction (in the Book of instruction) for how to build wisdom in our lives, and in our homes. The wisdom that has been passed through the generations of my family is an ever-example to how I want to live my life and raise my sons. I am glad we are able to share with you some of what we have found through our reading of this book, our experiences in life, and our love as a family.

 hapter 1

Proverbs 1
[1] The proverbs of Solomon the
son of David, king of Israel:
[2] To know wisdom and instruction,
To perceive the words of understanding,
[3] To receive the instruction of wisdom,
Justice, judgment, and equity;
[4] To give prudence to the simple,
To the young man knowledge and discretion—
[5] A wise man will hear and increase learning,
And a man of understanding will
attain wise counsel,
[6] To understand a proverb and an enigma,
The words of the wise and their riddles.
[7] The fear of the LORD is the beginning of
knowledge, But fools despise wisdom
and instruction.

Shun Evil Counsel
[8] My son, hear the instruction of your father,
And do not forsake the law of your mother;
[9] For they will be a graceful ornament on your
head, And chains about your neck.
[10] My son, if sinners entice you,
Do not consent.
[11] If they say, "Come with us,
Let us lie in wait to shed blood;
Let us lurk secretly for the
innocent without cause;
[12] Let us swallow them alive like Sheol,
And whole, like those who go down to the Pit;
[13] We shall find all kinds of precious possessions,
We shall fill our houses with spoil;
[14] Cast in your lot among us,
Let us all have one purse"—
[15] My son, do not walk in the
way with them,
Keep your foot from their path;
[16] For their feet run to evil,
And they make haste to shed blood.
[17] Surely, in vain the net is spread

In the sight of any bird;
¹⁸ But they lie in wait for their own blood,
They lurk secretly for their own lives.
¹⁹ So are the ways of everyone who is
greedy for gain;
It takes away the life of its owners.

The Call of Wisdom
²⁰ Wisdom calls aloud outside;
She raises her voice in the open squares.
²¹ She cries out in the chief concourses,
At the openings of the gates in the city
She speaks her words:
²² "How long, you simple ones,
will you love simplicity?
For scorners delight in their scorning,
And fools hate knowledge.
²³ Turn at my rebuke;
Surely I will pour out my spirit on you;
I will make my words known to you.
²⁴ Because I have called and you refused,
I have stretched out my hand and no
one regarded,
²⁵ Because you disdained all my counsel,
And would have none of my rebuke,
²⁶ I also will laugh at your calamity;
I will mock when your terror comes,
²⁷ When your terror comes like a storm,
And your destruction comes like a whirlwind,
When distress and anguish come upon you."
²⁸ Then they will call on me, but I will not
answer; They will seek me diligently, but
they will not find me.
²⁹ Because they hated knowledge
And did not choose the fear of the LORD,
³⁰ They would have none of my counsel
And despised my every rebuke.
³¹ Therefore they shall eat the fruit
of their own way,
And be filled to the full with
their own fancies.
³² For the turning away of the
simple will slay them,
And the complacency of
fools will destroy them;
³³ But whoever listens to me
will dwell safely,
And will be secure, without fear of evil.

In the Chapter
Wisdom is the Key Solomon Shared
We soon learn that the key word throughout the book is WISDOM. Solomon had a strong desire to know and understand wisdom and knowledge. He recognized these two treasures belonged together. He realized also that young men needed instruction to exercise justice and judgment (1:4).

We note immediately that God chose the proper person to be entrusted with the necessary qualities to create this book. Solomon knew that wise men would hear and apply the knowledge he also needed and received as a blessing from his Creator (1:5).

This pupil chosen by God recognized that the first quality people need is a fear of God, the Master Teacher. He states that is where knowledge begins (1:7). If we consider that first quality, we must understand immediately why we do not have a greater quantity of truly wise people today. Far too few fear God or recognize Him as Maker and Master. Too many are enticed by sinners rather than by our Savior. Solomon's wise directive is simply that we should refuse to listen to those who want to hinder rather than help us on our journey to true wisdom (1:8–19).

The key to this great masterpiece is wisdom; to open the lock of each chapter we must read in wisdom and be open to the knowledge and understanding that will come. We must come into God's presence with reverential fear, as we fear also (in a different way) ignorance.

Wisdom Shouts Out!
With interest we note wisdom is not lacking in the lives of men today because it is too hidden and too difficult to secure. Solomon teaches that wisdom shouts out (1:20)! Wisdom can be seen and heard. God doesn't ask us to seek the proverbial "needle in a haystack;" when we have eyes and a heart open, wisdom is as obvious as the haystack.

When we call for something detrimental or out of a contrary spirit, when we try to answer life's questions with only our desires, only then will wisdom become a faint, hard-to-find whisper. God says He will turn from us if we continue to turn from wisdom (1:28–30). Riches, which some misname as being valuable, and other desires of a selfish or stubborn heart can destroy us. Wisdom enables its owner to know the difference in what will bring value and what will bring destruction.

In Our Homes

A First Study
When I was first approached to co-author a book on Proverbs, I agreed, though recognizing the huge, serious undertaking. I recalled my first request to teach Proverbs while involved in work with the church in Bermuda many years ago. An elderly lady agreed to a personal study of the Bible and requested we study this book.

This was an eye-opening experience and a most rewarding one as well. Because of time limitations, I had to select some verses for each period of study. I'm sure I received more rewards than my elderly student did.

Since then I have had opportunities to present only single lessons on this book and have very often used passages to emphasize important points, but haven't since done an exclusive study into the book as I did that first time.

Parental Influence
One of the first great impressions made upon the serious reader is Solomon's admonition to heed good advice or counsel. He begins with a reference to wisdom, instruction, and understanding.

My personal observation for most of my life is that good people are taught by parents and peers to value these three qualities. However, some do not choose to make proper use of the good resources to make their goals in life to respect and follow such good advice.

In a few cases, good parents who usually offered good advice were unable to stamp moral and ethical values on the minds of their children. God's inspired penman specifically refers children "to receive the instruction of wisdom, justice, judgment, and equity" (1:3).

Sources of these qualities are usually parents, teachers, and close associates. I have noted that some who were exposed to such positive instruction at home allowed those they were closely associated with at school or work to overshadow the best advice.

It may be that some parents fail to exercise care in warning their charges to carefully choose their friends. In our modern days, I have noted that some parents do not even know their children's friends. One of my early blessings was the fact that my father and mother knew who my friends were and who their parents were.

An example is vivid still. When I was old enough to think about dating, my father learned who I was "running around with." When one girl's name came up, my dad was quick to advise me, "You can't date her; I know her parents." By that he simply meant her home life and family morals didn't align with ours. He knew such associates would hinder my growth and my reputation. Even much more serious results could come if I had begun to date someone whose family didn't hold to the value of wisdom held by my family. Thankfully I already had enough basic instruction and respect to know that Daddy was right!

Children are to receive a wise parent's instruction, and wise parents should be involved in the associations of their children, better ensuring the instruction at home stays with that child through life.

"There are many paths in life; wisdom enables us to choose the right one."

Chapter 2

Proverbs 2

The Value of Wisdom

¹ My son, if you receive my words,
   And treasure my commands within you,
² So that you incline your ear to wisdom,
   And apply your heart to understanding;
³ Yes, if you cry out for discernment,
   And lift up your voice for understanding,
⁴ If you seek her as silver,
   And search for her as for hidden treasures;
⁵ Then you will understand the fear of the
   LORD, And find the knowledge of God.
⁶ For the LORD gives wisdom; From His mouth
   come knowledge and understanding;
⁷ He stores up sound wisdom for the upright;
   He is a shield to those who walk uprightly;
⁸ He guards the paths of justice,
   And preserves the way of His saints.
⁹ Then you will understand
   righteousness and justice,
   Equity and every good path.
¹⁰ When wisdom enters your heart,
   And knowledge is pleasant to your soul,
¹¹ Discretion will preserve you;
   Understanding will keep you,
¹² To deliver you from the way of evil,
   From the man who speaks perverse things,
¹³ From those who leave the paths of uprightness
   To walk in the ways of darkness;
¹⁴ Who rejoice in doing evil,
   And delight in the perversity of the wicked;
¹⁵ Whose ways are crooked,
   And who are devious in their paths;
¹⁶ To deliver you from the immoral woman,
   From the seductress who flatters
   with her words,
¹⁷ Who forsakes the companion of her youth,
   And forgets the covenant of her God.
¹⁸ For her house leads down to death,
   And her paths to the dead;
¹⁹ None who go to her return,

Nor do they regain the paths of life—
[20] So you may walk in the way of goodness,
And keep to the paths of righteousness.
[21] For the upright will dwell in the land,
And the blameless will remain in it;
[22] But the wicked will be cut off from the earth,
And the unfaithful will be uprooted from it.

In the Chapter
True Wisdom and Riches
Chapter two reminds me not only to receive His word but to make it a part of my life. We must listen and apply God's ways to receive true riches, and not just the earthly definition of wealth, which is money or "silver" (2:4–5). Solomon reminds us that we need to properly understand the fearing of the Lord to gain wisdom (2:5).

Discerning the Right Path
There are many paths in life; wisdom enables us to choose the right one (2:9–15).

Our inspired penman associated words like discretion, mercy, truth, favor, knowledge, understanding, instruction, judgment, learning, righteousness, and preserve on the positive side of decision making and words like fools, despising, evil, forwardness, wicked, crooked, and transgressor on the negative side. The vast chasm between the two sides should help us to distinguish the truth and make wise choices.

In Our Homes
Fear the Lord
Solomon again refers to the importance of knowledge, wisdom, and understanding. He begins chapter two with the big-little word "if." He reminds, "if you will receive my words" (2:1) and continues with a reference to placing a high value on knowledge. In verse three reference is made to "fear of the Lord."

Why do children fear their earthly parents? Obviously the type of fear Solomon calls attention to is respect, honor, and love; trust is involved. The source of a fortunate child's wisdom emanates from Godly parents. Godly parents fear God in the proper way; their children fear both the Lord and their parents in the proper way as well. Generation after generation passes down this blessing of respect.

The proper fear taught and preserved in our homes brings other blessings, referred to in chapter two: understanding, wisdom, righteousness, equity, every good path, discretion, and deliverance, as mentioned earlier.

I am truly grateful that I was taught these blessings since my childhood.

 hapter 3

Proverbs 3

Guidance for the Young

1 My son, do not forget my law,
   But let your heart keep my commands;
2 For length of days and long life
   And peace they will add to you.
3 Let not mercy and truth forsake you;
   Bind them around your neck,
   Write them on the tablet of your heart,
4 And so find favor and high esteem
   In the sight of God and man.
5 Trust in the LORD with all your heart,
   And lean not on your own understanding;
6 In all your ways acknowledge Him,
   And He shall direct your paths.
7 Do not be wise in your own eyes;
   Fear the LORD and depart from evil.
8 It will be health to your flesh,
   And strength to your bones.
9 Honor the LORD with your possessions,
   And with the firstfruits of all your increase;
10 So your barns will be filled with plenty,
   And your vats will overflow with new wine.
11 My son, do not despise the chastening
   of the LORD,
   Nor detest His correction;
12 For whom the LORD loves He corrects,
   Just as a father the son in whom he delights.
13 Happy is the man who finds wisdom,
   And the man who gains understanding;
14 For her proceeds are better than the
   profits of silver,
   And her gain than fine gold.
15 She is more precious than rubies,
   And all the things you may desire
   cannot compare with her.
16 Length of days is in her right hand,
   In her left hand riches and honor.
17 Her ways are ways of pleasantness,
   And all her paths are peace.
18 She is a tree of life to those

who take hold of her,
And happy are all who retain her.

[19] The LORD by wisdom founded the earth;
By understanding He established the heavens;
[20] By His knowledge the depths were broken up,
And clouds drop down the dew.
[21] My son, let them not depart from your eyes—
Keep sound wisdom and discretion;
[22] So they will be life to your soul
And grace to your neck.
[23] Then you will walk safely in your way,
And your foot will not stumble.
[24] When you lie down, you will not be afraid;
Yes, you will lie down and your sleep
will be sweet.
[25] Do not be afraid of sudden terror,
Nor of trouble from the wicked when it comes;
[26] For the LORD will be your confidence,
And will keep your foot from being caught.
[27] Do not withhold good from those to whom
it is due,
When it is in the power
of your hand to do so.
[28] Do not say to your neighbor,
"Go, and come back,
And tomorrow I will give it,"
When you have it with you.
[29] Do not devise evil against your neighbor,
For he dwells by you for safety's sake.
[30] Do not strive with a man without cause,
If he has done you no harm.
[31] Do not envy the oppressor,
And choose none of his ways;
[32] For the perverse person is an
abomination to the LORD,
But His secret counsel is with the upright.
[33] The curse of the LORD is on the house
of the wicked,
But He blesses the home of the just.
[34] Surely He scorns the scornful,
But gives grace to the humble.
[35] The wise shall inherit glory,
But shame shall be the legacy of fools.

In the Chapter
Warnings and Rewards
This chapter begins with God's warnings and promises of reward. The first warning is that we must not forget God's law and should keep His commandments. The promise of reward will be a longer and more peaceful life (3:1–2).

Another warning is not to allow mercy and truth to escape us but to treat these blessings as a treasure. A reward for following this warning will be God's favor and understanding (3:3–4).

Then we are warned not to trust our own understanding but to trust in the Lord. If we do so, God will direct our paths (3:5–6).

Advice continues with us being told not to trust our own eyes but rather to fear the Lord and depart from evil (3:7). This is like God saying we shouldn't go our own way but His way. Our reward will be better health (3:8).

As strange as it may seem, Solomon's God-given wisdom allowed him to realize a need to honor God by giving back to Him; doing so will give the promised result of getting more in return (3:9–10).

The Creator reminds us that there will be some seemingly negative outcomes in life. There will be times of chastening. This, too, will be a reward as it can keep us on the right path, which would be a mark of the loving Father's love (3:11–12). Loving parents punish the children they love to correct, guide, and save them.

Happiness will be given to those of us who find true wisdom and understanding; such will be more valuable than any material merchandise (3:13–14). True riches and length of days are stressed again as a reward to we who possess and make proper use of our wisdom and wealth (3:15–18). The truly wise bless those around them.

Proverbs 3:19 reminds us that by wisdom God made the earth and the heaven; by His knowledge He keeps all under control. As the writer, directed by God, advises, we should not lose sight of all this evidence as we keep wisdom and discretion. Soul and body will be blessed by doing so (3:20–22). And if we follow the safe path free from stumbling, we can lie down and enjoy peaceful, sweet sleep (3:23–24). If we let God, He will be our confidence (3:25–26).

Further advice includes sharing our good blessings with those less fortunate. The Lord advises against striving with our neighbors and against envying the oppressor, or following his evil ways. The evil person is an abomination to the Lord and a curse on him (3:28–33). We can take comfort in knowing that the scornful will be scorned, but the lowly will receive grace. The wise will be glorified, and the fool will be shamed (3:34–35).

In Our Homes
Don't Forget God's Law
This wonderful chapter begins with a powerful admonition "forget not my law" (3:1). A number of valuable blessings attend the adherence to this plea. I was taught by my mother and daddy the necessity of knowing from where all my blessings originated. I was taught in my home to love, honor, and respect the Father of all and the Giver of all good things. God was held up as the final authority in all matters.

In raising our children, all parents would do well to often remind our children of our blessings, and the One who has given us those blessings. These reminders make us think of God, and thinking on His goodness in our lives can make it easier to follow Him. I do not find it in my nature to forget my God, His goodness and His laws, because I had this impressed on my mind in my home as a child.

 hapter 4

Proverbs 4
Security in Wisdom
¹ Hear, my children, the instruction of a father,
   And give attention to know understanding;
² For I give you good doctrine:
   Do not forsake my law.
³ When I was my father's son,
   Tender and the only one in
   the sight of my mother,
⁴ He also taught me, and said to me:
   "Let your heart retain my words;
   Keep my commands, and live.
⁵ Get wisdom! Get understanding!
   Do not forget, nor turn away from
   the words of my mouth.
⁶ Do not forsake her, and she
   will preserve you;
   Love her, and she will keep you.
⁷ Wisdom is the principal thing;
   Therefore get wisdom.
   And in all your getting, get understanding.
⁸ Exalt her, and she will promote you;
   She will bring you honor, when you
   embrace her.
⁹ She will place on your head
   an ornament of grace;
   A crown of glory she will deliver to you."
¹⁰ Hear, my son, and receive my sayings,
   And the years of your life will be many.
¹¹ I have taught you in the way of wisdom;
   I have led you in right paths.
¹² When you walk, your steps
   will not be hindered,
   And when you run, you will not stumble.
¹³ Take firm hold of instruction, do not let go;
   Keep her, for she is your life.
¹⁴ Do not enter the path of the wicked,
   And do not walk in the way of evil.
¹⁵ Avoid it, do not travel on it;
   Turn away from it and pass on.
¹⁶ For they do not sleep unless they

have done evil;
And their sleep is taken away
unless they make someone fall.
¹⁷ For they eat the bread of wickedness,
And drink the wine of violence.
¹⁸ But the path of the just is like the shining sun,
That shines ever brighter unto the perfect day.
¹⁹ The way of the wicked is like darkness;
They do not know what makes them stumble.
²⁰ My son, give attention to my words;
Incline your ear to my sayings.
²¹ Do not let them depart from your eyes;
Keep them in the midst of your heart;
²² For they are life to those who find them,
And health to all their flesh.
²³ Keep your heart with all diligence,
For out of it spring the issues of life.
²⁴ Put away from you a deceitful mouth,
And put perverse lips far from you.
²⁵ Let your eyes look straight ahead,
And your eyelids look right before you.
²⁶ Ponder the path of your feet,
And let all your ways be established.
²⁷ Do not turn to the right or the left;
Remove your foot from evil.

In the Chapter
From Parent to Child and On
Solomon advises children to hear the instruction of a wise father. In so doing they will gain understanding and enjoy good doctrine. His says advice and tender love came from his father and mother; he was taught to retain the wise words in his heart and keep the commandments of God (4:1–4). In turn, he teaches the ways of wisdom and leads us in the right paths (4:11).

Blessings from Wisdom
At verse five and seven, Solomon brings up wisdom again along with understanding. He further emphasizes the urgency of retaining wisdom and understanding and promises that if we love these things, the blessings that will come are safety, grace, a crown of glory, and a long, good life (4:6, 8–10).

When we walk or run in life, we will not stumble if we heed the advice of this wise writer (4:12). If we keep our eyes and ears open and store his wise advice in our hearts, the results will be health and life (4:20–22). Solomon promises that we should be wise listeners and diligently guard our hearts because that determines what life will be like (4:24–27).

Warning against the Wicked
The wise man's next sage advice: refrain from the path of the wicked and the way of evil men. We are told to not even pass by these people but to run away from them. The wicked never sleep unless they have done mischief and caused someone to stumble (4:14–16).

In verses seventeen through nineteen, the inspired man presents a contrast between the wicked and the just. The food and drink of the wicked is related to their violent natures. The path of the just is comparable to a shining light that grows brighter and brighter as they go through life, by way of contrast to the darkness of the wicked as they stumble through life (4:20–22).

In Our Homes
Results of Disobedience and Obedience
This chapter presents the reason some disobey His will; it also looks at the results of disobedience in contrast to the positive results for obedience.

Parents will do well to follow this example in our homes. I am thankful that both my parents and my wife's parents rewarded us with positive responses when we obeyed and punished us for disrespect and disobedience. Being raised in this way made it more natural for us as parents when we tried to apply God's system of reward and punishment in our home.

It is also very profitable to recognize the desired results of respect and obedience to both our Heavenly Father and our earthly parents. Our home life should prepare us for our heavenly home.

 hapter 5

Proverbs 5
The Peril of Adultery

[1] My son, pay attention to my wisdom;
  Lend your ear to my understanding,
[2] That you may preserve discretion,
  And your lips may keep knowledge.
[3] For the lips of an immoral woman drip honey,
  And her mouth is smoother than oil;
[4] But in the end she is bitter as wormwood,
  Sharp as a two-edged sword.
[5] Her feet go down to death,
  Her steps lay hold of hell.
[6] Lest you ponder her path of life—
  Her ways are unstable;
  You do not know them.
[7] Therefore hear me now, my children,
  And do not depart from the words
  of my mouth.
[8] Remove your way far from her,
  And do not go near the door of her house,
[9] Lest you give your honor to others,
  And your years to the cruel one;
[10] Lest aliens be filled with your wealth,
  And your labors go to the house of
  a foreigner;
[11] And you mourn at last,
  When your flesh and your
  body are consumed,
[12] And say:
  "How I have hated instruction,
  And my heart despised correction!
[13] I have not obeyed the voice of my teachers,
  Nor inclined my ear to those who
  instructed me!
[14] I was on the verge of total ruin,
  In the midst of the assembly
  and congregation."
[15] Drink water from your own cistern,
  And running water from your own well.
[16] Should your fountains be dispersed abroad,
  Streams of water in the streets?

17 Let them be only your own,
   And not for strangers with you.
18 Let your fountain be blessed,
   And rejoice with the wife of your youth.
19 As a loving deer and a graceful doe,
   Let her breasts satisfy you at all times;
   And always be enraptured with her love.
20 For why should you, my son, be
   enraptured by an immoral woman,
   And be embraced in the arms
   of a seductress?
21 For the ways of man are
   before the eyes of the LORD,
   And He ponders all his paths.
22 His own iniquities entrap the wicked man,
   And he is caught in the cords of his sin.
23 He shall die for lack of instruction,
   And in the greatness of his folly he
   shall go astray.

In the Chapter
Watch Out for the Evil Woman
With all urgency, in Proverbs 5:1–6 Solomon enlists careful attention to his wisdom and his understanding in order that regard for discretion would result and knowledge could be embraced. Immediately he follows that we should apply caution when evil women with enticing words attempt to deceive and rob of purity. He uses two strong expressions to warn of the result of rejecting his advice: the outcome will be "bitter as wormwood and dangerous as a two-edged sword" (5:4). Further outcome will be death and hell.

Punishment for Ignoring the Wise Advice
Such great advise and warning would be priceless to youth in any age. We should not even consider a sweet, tempting offer for it is deceiving beyond knowledge. To refuse the well-intended advice will be allowing ourselves to be tied with the strong cords of sin. Without advice of the proper kind, received and applied fully, the innocent will surely be lead astray, sacrificing honor and resulting in cruel years (5:7–9).

Further results of improper action and sinful, immoral conduct are like allowing strangers to consume our wealth; our health will decline and our bodies be consumed (5: 10 –11). Too late the conclusion might be reached that good instruction had been rejected, and that we had refused the advice of good teachers. We have to be careful because, even if we are surrounded by good people in the assembly, if we are disobedient, we will be severely punished (5:12 –14).

Abstain from Adultery
We must live a good life guided by the instructions of wise teachers and be faithful to the wife of our youth. We are told to abstain from adultery, to enjoy a lifetime of faithful love and enjoy the marriage honored and blessed by God: the honor of a mutual faithful relationship. Solomon says to be mindful of the fact that the Lord knows all about our lives and our relationships (5:15–23).

In Our Homes

Guarding Our Lives
Our heavenly Father prepared us for life here and hereafter. Parents have a God-given responsibility to teach children that God blesses us in that way. This teaching includes warnings against immoral people who will attempt to deceive us into accepting their evil lifestyles.

If our children are taught these truths and receive these warnings, better, long-lasting results will follow. If such information is not given in our homes, our children may learn the hard way too late.

Under an interesting saying, Solomon warns against adulterous relationships by saying "drink water from your own cistern" meaning we must satisfy our sexual desires with our own God-accepted mate (5:15). This lesson must be taught to our children; we must be a good example.

Faithful parents can best teach their children to be faithful partners.

hapter 6

Proverbs 6

Dangerous Promises

1 My son, if you become
   surety for your friend,
   If you have shaken hands
   in pledge for a stranger,
2 You are snared by the
   words of your mouth;
   You are taken by the
   words of your mouth.
3 So do this, my son,
   and deliver yourself;
   For you have come into
   the hand of your friend:
   Go and humble yourself;
   Plead with your friend.
4 Give no sleep to your eyes,
   Nor slumber to your eyelids.
5 Deliver yourself like a gazelle
   from the hand of the hunter,
   And like a bird from the hand
   of the fowler.

The Folly of Indolence

6 Go to the ant, you sluggard!
   Consider her ways and be wise,
7 Which, having no captain,
   Overseer, or ruler,
8 Provides her supplies in the summer,
   And gathers her food in the harvest.
9 How long will you slumber, O sluggard?
   When will you rise from your sleep?
10 A little sleep, a little slumber,
   A little folding of the hands to sleep—
11 So shall your poverty come on you
   like a prowler,
   And your need like an armed man.

The Wicked Man

12 A worthless person, a wicked man,
   Walks with a perverse mouth;

¹³ He winks with his eyes,
   He shuffles his feet,
   He points with his fingers;
¹⁴ Perversity is in his heart,
   He devises evil continually,
   He sows discord.
¹⁵ Therefore his calamity shall come suddenly;
   Suddenly he shall be broken without remedy.
¹⁶ These six things the LORD hates,
   Yes, seven are an abomination to Him:
¹⁷ A proud look,
   A lying tongue,
   Hands that shed innocent blood,
¹⁸ A heart that devises wicked plans,
   Feet that are swift in running to evil,
¹⁹ A false witness who speaks lies,
   And one who sows discord among brethren.

Beware of Adultery
²⁰ My son, keep your father's command,
   And do not forsake the law of your mother.
²¹ Bind them continually upon your heart;
   Tie them around your neck.
²² When you roam, they will lead you;
   When you sleep, they will keep you;
   And when you awake, they will speak with you.
²³ For the commandment is a lamp,
   And the law a light;
   Reproofs of instruction are the way of life,
²⁴ To keep you from the evil woman,
   From the flattering tongue of a seductress.
²⁵ Do not lust after her beauty in your heart,
   Nor let her allure you with her eyelids.
²⁶ For by means of a harlot
   A man is reduced to a crust of bread;
   And an adulteress will prey upon his
   precious life.
²⁷ Can a man take fire to his bosom,
   And his clothes not be burned?
²⁸ Can one walk on hot coals,
   And his feet not be seared?
²⁹ So is he who goes in to his neighbor's wife;
   Whoever touches her shall not be innocent.
³⁰ People do not despise a thief
   If he steals to satisfy himself
   when he is starving.
³¹ Yet when he is found, he must
   restore seven fold;
   He may have to give up all the substance

of his house.
32 Whoever commits adultery with a
woman lacks understanding;
He who does so destroys his own soul.
33 Wounds and dishonor he will get,
And his reproach will not be wiped away.
34 For jealousy is a husband's fury;
Therefore he will not spare in the
day of vengeance.
35 He will accept no recompense,
Nor will he be appeased though you
give many gifts.

In the Chapter
Guard Your Body
Solomon's wise advice to a son includes the exercise of extreme care in the use of the tongue. He compares the careless words of the mouth to a trap, thus impressing the danger of unguarded words (6:1–2). Naughty and wicked people are those who talk too much and who use eyes, feet, and fingers to accomplish mischief and sow discord, but their actions will bring unexpected destruction (6:12–15).

Solomon lists seven things that the Lord hates and which result in abomination in His sight. It is notable that most are body members and their sinful acts. The list includes proud eyes, a lying tongue, hands that shed innocent blood, a heart that devises wicked imagination, feet that are swift in running to mischief, a fake witness that lies, and one who stirs up trouble among others (6:16–19) Obviously our Creator hates the misuse of any of the senses or members of our body. He created the body to be used to honor Him, not to hinder others also made in His image.

One of the designs and purposes of this chapter on wisdom is to enable us to guard against the devil's appeals to the lusts of the flesh. Special attention is given to the young who may be easily tempted by the seductive woman. With descriptive detail Solomon calls attention to evil women's methods of appeal. She will use her overall beauty; her evil, flattering tongue; her facial expressions; and her mannerisms. The outcome of falling to her charms will be the loss of purity and prosperity (6:24–26). If a man is seduced into adultery, he will feel horrible guilt, receive dishonor and reproach that cannot be removed, and even experience the destruction of his soul (6:29, 32–35).

Be Alert, Not Asleep
The advice continues as Solomon says we shouldn't spend too much time in sleep and should awaken from lazy habits (6:4, 9–11). We should be alert as a deer is when danger is present (6:5). Or, another animal example, sluggards are told to learn a valuable, dear lesson from the small but industrious ant. This insect works hard and needs no boss to guide or force him into making preparation for the future while time and opportunity is available (6:6–8).

Solomon mentions sleep again when he explains that the wise man has proper respect for his parents; the writer paints a vivid picture of binding the advice of parents in the heart and around the neck, carrying them with us wherever we go, if asleep or awake (6:20–22).

In Our Homes
Every Body
As parents, we need to teach our children to know what God approves of, but also what He hates. Our wise Father saw fit to inspire Solomon to warn readers regarding purity of our bodies. Both God and Solomon obviously knew one of our greatest temptations would be associated with protection of our bodies. This includes guarding our innocence, and also other areas. Our bodies are made in His image, and we should care for them in all respects: with exercise, good nutrition, and purity. We must teach our children to take care of their bodies as they consider them a gift from their Creator; one of the best ways to teach is to live by example as we are careful with our own bodies, showing respect to our Father in this way.

Working Hard is Hard Work
Careful homes will prepare children to grow up and be diligent and industrious. We can learn

from nature's hardworking examples. If we are to tell our children not to be lazy, though, we must practice this advice by word and by example.

Living a life that is reflective of the lessons we teach will make us worthy of the respect of our children. They are told to revere and heed our advice, but that doesn't mean we can speak one way and live another. If we want hardworking children, we must be hardworking parents.

"Well-loved Bibles show their wear."

hapter 7

Proverbs 7

[1] My son, keep my words,
 And treasure my
 commands within you.
[2] Keep my commands and live,
 And my law as the
 apple of your eye.
[3] Bind them on your fingers;
 Write them on the
 tablet of your heart.
[4] Say to wisdom,
 "You are my sister,"
 And call understanding
 your nearest kin,
[5] That they may keep you
 from the immoral woman,
 From the seductress who
 flatters with her words.

The Crafty Harlot
[6] For at the window of my house
 I looked through my lattice,
[7] And saw among the simple,
 I perceived among the youths,
 A young man devoid of understanding,
[8] Passing along the street near her corner;
 And he took the path to her house
[9] In the twilight, in the evening,
 In the black and dark night.
[10] And there a woman met him,
 With the attire of a harlot,
 and a crafty heart.
[11] She was loud and rebellious,
 Her feet would not stay at home.
[12] At times she was outside, at times
 in the open square,
 Lurking at every corner.
[13] So she caught him and kissed him;
 With an impudent face she said to him:
[14] "I have peace offerings with me;
 Today I have paid my vows.

¹⁵ So I came out to meet you,
   Diligently to seek your face,
   And I have found you.
¹⁶ I have spread my bed with tapestry,
   Colored coverings of Egyptian linen.
¹⁷ I have perfumed my bed
   With myrrh, aloes, and cinnamon.
¹⁸ Come, let us take our fill of love until morning;
   Let us delight ourselves with love.
¹⁹ For my husband is not at home;
   He has gone on a long journey;
²⁰ He has taken a bag of money with him,
   And will come home on the appointed day."
²¹ With her enticing speech she caused
   him to yield,
   With her flattering lips she seduced him.
²² Immediately he went after her, as an ox goes
   to the slaughter,
   Or as a fool to the correction of the stocks,
²³ Till an arrow struck his liver.
   As a bird hastens to the snare,
   He did not know it would cost his life.
²⁴ Now therefore, listen to me, my children;
   Pay attention to the words of my mouth:
²⁵ Do not let your heart turn aside to her ways,
   Do not stray into her paths;
²⁶ For she has cast down many wounded,
   And all who were slain by her were strong men.
²⁷ Her house is the way to hell,
   Descending to the chambers of death.

In the Chapter
Men in Wisdom with Women

This chapter focuses mainly on the topic of a man's relationship with women. The marvelous wisdom of Solomon is employed to appeal to his son to remember and keep his words, to attach them to his physical being and heart. He presents the idea of wisdom being like a sister, as close as a dear relative (7:1–4).

Then he begins to talk about a different type of relationship with a woman; juxtaposed to the talk about a dear sister, he begins to talk about an adulterous woman.

Our inspired penman describes looking through his window and seeing a young man, lacking in understanding, going near the sinful woman's house. In the darkness of the night the young man meets with the harlot, experienced in the art of seduction. She is prepared to tempt him and take advantage of his desire and lack of wisdom. She uses kisses, her facial expressions, and her voice to attract him with exactly what she knows will appeal to the lusts of the flesh; she promises him a night of satisfaction and assures him her husband is away, so they will not be disturbed (7:6–21).

Solomon then pictures the young man being deceived as he focuses on one thing—a night of physical pleasure—and therefore follows the wicked woman. The young man is compared to an ox going to the slaughter, a fool on his way to the stocks, or a bird rushing to the snare, unaware it is going to its death (7:22–23).

The young man in danger is urged to listen and carefully heed this warning: refuse to listen to the harlot, and do not accept her invitation. Those who did accept her enticing words were wounded or lost their lives; her house is compared to death and hell (7:24–27).

In Our Homes
Love in Another Direction
In the best homes one will find at least one Bible that has, from its appearance, obviously been used regularly. Well-loved Bibles show their wear.

A few years ago a very dear friend died unexpectedly. He was a local newspaper editor and owner, well respected even by people who didn't always agree with him. Hundreds of people attended a very long service, and no one complained.

His youngest son read some passages from his dad's Bible. Then the son held the well-worn book up for all to see. His comments were, "This is the way a Bible ought to look." The cover was worn completely off, and the pages were marked up with notes written throughout.

When I read Proverbs chapter seven, I was reminded of Bob's Bible. Solomon advised that his son keep God's word with him. He stated this would keep him out of trouble. He said to treat the Bible as a sister. Then I thought about how my dear friend's family loved their Bibles as God's word indeed. As a result, they loved the Lord and served Him.

We will be enticed to passion in life; why not let that passion be directed towards a love of God's Word and His ways. Then, instead of fear of death and hell as a result of filling inappropriate desires, we can have the hope of heaven.

 hapter 8

Proverbs 8
The Excellence of Wisdom
1 Does not wisdom cry out,
  And understanding lift up her voice?
2 She takes her stand on the top of the high hill,
  Beside the way, where the paths meet.
3 She cries out by the gates, at the
  entry of the city,
  At the entrance of the doors:
4 "To you, O men, I call,
  And my voice is to the sons of men.
5 O you simple ones, understand prudence,
  And you fools, be of an understanding heart.
6 Listen, for I will speak of excellent things,
  And from the opening of my lips will
  come right things;
7 For my mouth will speak truth;
  Wickedness is an abomination to my lips.
8 All the words of my mouth are with
  righteousness;
  Nothing crooked or perverse is in them.
9 They are all plain to him who understands,
  And right to those who find knowledge.
10 Receive my instruction, and not silver,
  And knowledge rather than choice gold;
11 For wisdom is better than rubies,
  And all the things one may desire
  cannot be compared with her.
12 I, wisdom, dwell with prudence,
  And find out knowledge and discretion.
13 The fear of the LORD is to hate evil;
  Pride and arrogance and the evil way
  And the perverse mouth I hate.
14 Counsel is mine, and sound wisdom;
  I am understanding, I have strength.
15 By me kings reign,
  And rulers decree justice.
16 By me princes rule, and nobles,
  All the judges of the earth.
17 I love those who love me,
  And those who seek me diligently will find me.

¹⁸ Riches and honor are with me,
   Enduring riches and righteousness.
¹⁹ My fruit is better than gold, yes, than fine gold,
   And my revenue than choice silver.
²⁰ I traverse the way of righteousness,
   In the midst of the paths of justice,
²¹ That I may cause those who love me
   to inherit wealth,
   That I may fill their treasuries.
²² The LORD possessed me at the
   beginning of His way,
   Before His works of old.
²³ I have been established from everlasting,
   From the beginning, before there was
   ever an earth.
²⁴ When there were no
   depths I was brought forth,
   When there were no
   fountains abounding with water.
²⁵ Before the mountains were settled,
   Before the hills, I was brought forth;
²⁶ While as yet He had not made the earth
   or the fields,
   Or the primal dust of the world.
²⁷ When He prepared the heavens, I was there,
   When He drew a circle on the face of the deep,
²⁸ When He established the clouds above,
   When He strengthened the fountains
   of the deep,
²⁹ When He assigned to
   the sea its limit,
   So that the waters
   would not transgress
   His command,
   When He marked out
   the foundations of the earth,
³⁰ Then I was beside Him as a master craftsman;
   And I was daily His delight,
   Rejoicing always before Him,
³¹ Rejoicing in His inhabited world,
   And my delight was with the sons of men.
³² Now therefore, listen to me, my children,
   For blessed are those who keep my ways.
³³ Hear instruction and be wise,
   And do not disdain it.
³⁴ Blessed is the man who listens to me,
   Watching daily at my gates,
   Waiting at the posts of my doors.
³⁵ For whoever finds me finds life,

And obtains favor from the LORD;
³⁶ But he who sins against me wrongs
his own soul;
All those who hate me love death."

In the Chapter

Wisdom is Obvious and Directive

Solomon pictures wisdom making itself so obvious it is as though its voice cries out at the gates and along the paths; understanding wisdom will lend a voice to its message, as it is personified at the beginning of this chapter as a woman announcing her clear message to the young, pleading for them to understand and heed her warning (8:1–5). She promises excellent things and direction to right choices (8:6), and she promises to speak the truth, as opposed to wickedness or abomination; words of wisdom are the truth and are conducive to righteousness as opposed to false and perverse actions (8:7).

Wisdom is plain to those who wish to understand and accept knowledge (8:8–9), and it is more valuable than silver or gold or rubies or any other material thing that we might desire or lust after (8:10–11, 19). God can enable us to use our possessions wisely and become even more blessed, if we will embrace these truths and exercise Godly attitudes in blessing others (8:19–21). True riches and honor belong to God; durable riches and righteousness come from Him. What a blessing all would enjoy if the rich and powerful believed so and used their blessings guided by His ways (8:18).

Companions of Wisdom

Wisdom enjoys the companionship with prudence and the knowledge of witty inventions (8:12). The reverential fear of the Lord requires hating those things the Lord disapproves of. Some are listed to clarify: pride, arrogance, evil ways, and a foul mouth (8:13). These things do not go along with wisdom; instead, we should be sound, understanding, and strong if we are to live wise lives (8:14).

Just ruling is another companion to wisdom. Those entrusted with power to rule others must recognize that God allows such power but that He is over even those in authority, so they should deal the judgment God would approve of (8:16). God exercises a great degree of love for those who love Him and His ways and assists those who allow Him to do His will in their lives (8:17).

The Creator and His Creation
The Creator, God who made all things, including time, also made us and has a plan for all He made including us. He prepared all things and had all needs provided for before man was even created. He specifies the heavens, the seas, the clouds, the foundations of the earth—all made to conform to humanity's needs (8:22–26).

God continues to establish His eternal nature and the fact that He is still in control, reminding us of His unlimited power and His awareness of mankind; He is delighted when we allow Him to control our lives (8:27–31).

Our wise informer, Solomon, instructs us to be aware of His works, love, and expectations of us. He instructs us to listen to our Creator, to whom we are deeply indebted, and he pronounces a blessing on those who do so. Those who recognize our Father (in how we live) shall find His favor (8:32 –35).

In Our Homes
It has been my delightful experience to visit in many, many homes through the years. The home visits were made in several states and some even outside of this country. It was obvious that some of these homes exuded joy, contentment, peace, and hospitality. In others these qualities were noticeably lacking. As I took time to consider the question of "Why the difference?" one answer kept coming to the forefront.

In some of these homes love flowed for family members. Care for other family members was displayed. The name of God came up in conversations. Prayers of thanks were a natural pre-meal habit. One or more copies of the Word of God was visible, and good religious books were openly found.

In the other homes, God's name was never mentioned, neither were prayers offered up. Religious topics were taboo. No religious rituals occurred. Wisdom and understanding were sparse. The closest thing to worship was in regard to items of wealth.

I am reminded of Solomon's evaluation in Proverbs 8:11. "For wisdom is better than rubies; and all the things that may be desired are not to be compared to it."

We must be sure that God's wisdom, shown in part by a gratefulness for His creation of us and the blessings around us and also in our treatment of our family members, is obvious both in our hearts and in our homes.

 hapter 9

Proverbs 9
The Way of Wisdom
[1] Wisdom has built her house,
   She has hewn out her seven pillars;
[2] She has slaughtered her meat,
   She has mixed her wine,
   She has also furnished her table.
[3] She has sent out her maidens,
   She cries out from the highest places
   of the city,
[4] "Whoever is simple, let him turn in here!"
   As for him who lacks understanding,
   she says to him,
[5] "Come, eat of my bread
   And drink of the wine I have mixed.
[6] Forsake foolishness and live,
   And go in the way of understanding."
[7] He who corrects a scoffer gets shame
   for himself,
   And he who rebukes a
   wicked man only harms himself.
[8] Do not correct a scoffer, lest he hate you;
   Rebuke a wise man, and he will love you.
[9] Give instruction to a wise man, and he will
   be still wiser;
   Teach a just man, and he
   will increase in learning.
[10] "The fear of the LORD is
   the beginning of wisdom,
   And the knowledge of the
   Holy One is understanding.
[11] For by me your days will be multiplied,
   And years of life will be added to you.
[12] If you are wise, you are wise for yourself,
   And if you scoff, you will bear it alone."

The Way of Folly
[13] A foolish woman is clamorous;
   She is simple, and knows nothing.
[14] For she sits at the door of her house,
   On a seat by the highest places of the city,

¹⁵ To call to those who pass by,
 Who go straight on their way:
¹⁶ "Whoever is simple, let him turn in here;"
 And as for him who lacks understanding,
 she says to him,
¹⁷ "Stolen water is sweet,
 And bread eaten in secret is pleasant."
¹⁸ But he does not know that the dead are there,
 That her guests are in the depths of hell.

In the Chapter
Wisdom as a Hostess
Our master instructor, armed with inspiration from God, gives us further instruction and information about wisdom. He emphasizes that wisdom has made all necessary preparation and provision for the building and provisions of her house. The materials for the house and the food for a feast have been selected and carefully made ready; when all is completely ready, she sends forth her maidens to extend a welcome invitation to her guests, who are people who desire understanding (9:1–4).

The attractive menu includes bread and drink lovingly prepared (9:5). Those who come to the feast, who forsake foolish things, are promised life and understanding (9:6). Since wisdom is personified as a wealthy hostess extending a gracious invitation to people in need, we would expect that wisdom advises that which is the best.

Correct Correction
Our attempts to correct the scornful may repay us with personal harm. On the other hand, when we correct a wise man we may be repaid with love for our concern. The wise man will become ever wiser because we love him enough to instruct him. When we teach just people, they will increase their knowledge of truth (9:7–9). It is interested that our love for another, which prompts correction, benefits both the helper and the one helped, but the foolish does not profit and may also be hindered from our advice, because he cannot see past his foolishness to understand its value.

Gifts of Wisdom
Fear of the Lord is a successful step toward wisdom. Understanding grows with knowledge of God. A gift of using wisdom and knowledge is a longer, better life. The happiness and success of the wise grow alongside the wisdom (9:10 –11). The wise are profited by many benefits, now and eternally, while the scoffer (who rejects wisdom) will be punished (9:12). It seems that the indication is that wisdom and knowledge go beyond this physical existence.

The Foolish Woman: an Example of How NOT to Be
The foolish woman is one of those who possesses no regard for wisdom. As a result she appeals to others who are unwise and offers physical pleasure (which is short lived) and tempts the one who lacks wisdom with the temptations of the flesh; she can offer nothing of lasting value (9:13).

The foolish, sinful woman places herself in a noticeable position and invites and attracts the foolish passersby to partake of the short-term pleasure, and the simple are taken in and sell their souls to the devil (9:14–16). She offers what seems to be sweet, pleasant, and satisfying, when in reality she robs those who lack wisdom, filling them with lust that will satisfy for the moment but rob for eternity (9:17). Solomon warns again that those overcome by present, temporary pleasures will not consider the eternal outcome; guests of the temptress are already dead (9:18).

In Our Homes
Building Our Homes in Wisdom
In chapter nine the wise scribe of Proverbs personifies wisdom as a builder and gracious hostess. First there is the selection of the best materials and the best construction; then there is the preparation of the best foods and the invitation being sent out for guests to come. The guests are not those who are necessarily the richest and wisest, but those who seek better things in life (9:1–4)

To be wise today, we must plan our houses, our homes, well—both figuratively and literally. We use good materials and erect the house properly on sound foundations of wisdom and reverential fear of the Creator. We make it a home by also using that which is conducive to health and happiness of all members of those who live there. The good and wise exercise hospitality and share what we have been blessed with. The guests who heed our invitation are benefited by coming to our homes and sharing in the physical and spiritual blessings we have.

hapter 10

Proverbs 10
Wise Sayings of Solomon
[1] The proverbs of Solomon:
   A wise son makes a glad father,
   But a foolish son is the grief of his mother.
[2] Treasures of wickedness profit nothing,
   But righteousness delivers from death.
[3] The LORD will not allow the righteous
   soul to famish,
   But He casts away the desire of the wicked.
[4] He who has a slack hand becomes poor,
   But the hand of the diligent makes rich.
[5] He who gathers in summer is a wise son;
   He who sleeps in harvest is a son who
   causes shame.
[6] Blessings are on the head of the righteous,
   But violence covers the mouth of the wicked.
[7] The memory of the righteous is blessed,
   But the name of the wicked will rot.
[8] The wise in heart will receive commands,
   But a prating fool will fall.
[9] He who walks with integrity walks securely,
   But he who perverts his ways will become
   known.
[10] He who winks with the eye causes trouble,
   But a prating fool will fall.
[11] The mouth of the righteous is a well of life,
   But violence covers the mouth of the wicked.
[12] Hatred stirs up strife,
   But love covers all sins.
[13] Wisdom is found on the lips of him
   who has understanding,
   But a rod is for the back of him who is
   devoid of understanding.
[14] Wise people store up knowledge,
   But the mouth of the foolish is
   near destruction.
[15] The rich man's wealth is his strong city;
   The destruction of the poor is their poverty.
[16] The labor of the righteous leads to life,
   The wages of the wicked to sin.

17 He who keeps instruction is in the way of life,
   But he who refuses correction goes astray.
18 Whoever hides hatred has lying lips,
   And whoever spreads slander is a fool.
19 In the multitude of words sin is not lacking,
   But he who restrains his lips is wise.
20 The tongue of the righteous is choice silver;
   The heart of the wicked is worth little.
21 The lips of the righteous feed many,
   But fools die for lack of wisdom.
22 The blessing of the LORD makes one rich,
   And He adds no sorrow with it.
23 To do evil is like sport to a fool,
   But a man of understanding has wisdom.
24 The fear of the wicked will come upon him,
   And the desire of the righteous will
   be granted.
25 When the whirlwind passes by,
   the wicked is no more,
   But the righteous has an
   everlasting foundation.
26 As vinegar to the teeth and smoke to the eyes,
   So is the lazy man to those who send him.
27 The fear of the LORD prolongs days,
   But the years of the wicked will be shortened.
28 The hope of the righteous will be gladness,
   But the expectation of the wicked will perish.
29 The way of the LORD is strength for
   the upright,
   But destruction will come to the
   workers of iniquity.
30 The righteous will never be removed,
   But the wicked will not inhabit the earth.
31 The mouth of the righteous brings
   forth wisdom,
   But the perverse tongue will be cut out.
32 The lips of the righteous know what
   is acceptable,
   But the mouth of the wicked what is perverse.

In the Chapter
Teach Well; Learn Well

Solomon seems to be writing not only as a teacher to his students but also as a father to his children. He writes from the perspective that the father teaches the children proper values; one objective of good children is to honor and respect good parents. Those who do so honor and please their parents. Those who do not bring misery to their fathers and mothers (10:1).

Wise people will, by nature, receive commandments and apply them wisely, gaining good results (10:8). Those who walk the right pathway can walk safely and securely. Proper morals will guide in choosing the way and in the attitude with which we go through life. Those who choose the wrong path will follow that crooked way and reap a bad name and unpleasant destinations (10:9).

Wise men collect knowledge as a valuable treasure. Quite the contrary is the mouth of the foolish person who draws closer to destruction every day (10:14). If we follow good instructions, we walk the higher, better road of life. If we reject or refuse to take constructive criticism, we will experience the results of many mistakes (10:17).

Wealth from Where?
Ill-gotten gain, no matter how much the monetary value may be, brings misery to our loved ones; on the other hand, righteous lives produce a longer, happier existence (10:2–3). Though wealthy by earthly standard, one who has obtained his wealth by sinful acts will become poor by proper standards (10:4).

Material wealth is very deceptive. Those who possess it may take comfort in the power they think wealth will afford. On the other hand, the poor may be destroyed by their attitude towards wealth as well. They may give up out of misery, sunken spirits, or a failure to cultivate a sense of gratitude for what they do possess, feeling sorry for themselves and failing to recognize opportunities (10:15).

Actions and Effects
If we plan ahead and carefully execute good plans, we show wisdom. However, if we are careless and do not plan or work but are lazy, we will harvest shameful results (10:5). All true blessings are from above, and if we realize this and conduct our lives worthily, we will enjoy showers of blessings (10:6).

A righteous man speaks from a good heart, and his motives and actions will benefit others. The motives and acts of a violent man may be hidden by his sweet talk, but he cannot completely cover the wickedness of his true intentions (10:11).

If we practice excessive speaking, we are more likely to sin; we would be wise to control our speech (10:19). Furthermore, the speech of just people is comparable to valuable silver, while the heart of the wicked person is of little value (10:27). "As a man thinks in his heart, so is he" (23:7). The lips of the righteous help meet the needs of many people; those who fail to control their tongues bring pain to many and will suffer themselves as well (10:21).

Hatred not only affects the life of its owner, but it disturbs the lives of all who are exposed to it. Love not only determines our thoughts and touches our lives, but also has a part in the lives of all we associate with. Love prevents, cures, excuses, covers, erases, forgives, overlooks, corrects, rejects, and more—to turn bad into good (10:12)! I am reminded in this passage of another, where the Apostle Paul concludes in I Corinthians 13:13 that love is even greater than faith and hope.

If we are righteous, our hope and gladness will be fulfilled, while the wicked person's expectations will be disappointed (10:28). If we are righteous, we will build a rewarding life here and eternally, while the wicked person shall experience bitter consequences here and after (10:29–30).

In Our Homes
Here and Beyond
In the Christian home today we parents love and take pride in our children. We teach our children true values; the merits of hard, honest work; and the use of our minds to instill more moral values. When our children grow up, acquire a proper education, and become gainfully employed in moral professions, we are thankful. We still expect them to practice the standards we taught them. We want our children to cherish always happy memories of home.

The wise, thankful child walks uprightly and keeps the commandments of God that were taught to him at home, making his parents proud and happy. If parents have not exercised moral judgments or if the offspring become untrue to their upbringing, parents will be left with a heavy heart.

The wisdom of Solomon, when appreciated in our homes, extends far beyond our homes.

 hapter 11

Proverbs 11

1 Dishonest scales are an
   abomination to the LORD,
   But a just weight is His delight.
2 When pride comes, then comes shame;
   But with the humble is wisdom.
3 The integrity of the upright will guide them,
   But the perversity of the unfaithful will
   destroy them.
4 Riches do not profit in the day of wrath,
   But righteousness delivers from death.
5 The righteousness of the blameless will
   direct his way aright,
   But the wicked will fall
   by his own wickedness.
6 The righteousness of the
   upright will deliver them,
   But the unfaithful will be
   caught by their lust.
7 When a wicked man dies,
   his expectation will perish,
   And the hope of the unjust perishes.
8 The righteous is delivered from trouble,
   And it comes to the wicked instead.
9 The hypocrite with his mouth
   destroys his neighbor,
   But through knowledge
   the righteous will be delivered.
10 When it goes well with the
    righteous, the city rejoices;
    And when the wicked perish,
    there is jubilation.
11 By the blessing of the
    upright the city is exalted,
    But it is overthrown by the
    mouth of the wicked.
12 He who is devoid of
    wisdom despises his neighbor,
    But a man of understanding
    holds his peace.
13 A talebearer reveals secrets,

But he who is of a faithful
spirit conceals a matter.
¹⁴ Where there is no counsel,
the people fall;
But in the multitude of
counselors there is safety.
¹⁵ He who is surety for a stranger will suffer,
But one who hates being surety is secure.
¹⁶ A gracious woman retains honor,
But ruthless men retain riches.
¹⁷ The merciful man does good for his own soul,
But he who is cruel troubles his own flesh.
¹⁸ The wicked man does deceptive work,
But he who sows righteousness will
have a sure reward.
¹⁹ As righteousness leads to life,
So he who pursues evil pursues
it to his own death.
²⁰ Those who are of a perverse heart
are an abomi-nation to the LORD,
But the blameless in their ways are
His delight.
²¹ Though they join forces, the
wicked will not go unpunished;
But the posterity of the righteous
will be delivered.
²² As a ring of gold in a swine's snout,
So is a lovely woman who lacks discretion.
²³ The desire of the righteous is only good,
But the expectation of the wicked is wrath.
²⁴ There is one who scatters,
yet increases more;
And there is one who
withholds more than is right,
But it leads to poverty.
²⁵ The generous soul will be made rich,
And he who waters will also be
watered himself.
²⁶ The people will curse
him who withholds grain,
But blessing will be on the
head of him who sells it.
²⁷ He who earnestly seeks good finds favor,
But trouble will come to him who seeks evil.
²⁸ He who trusts in his riches will fall,
But the righteous will flourish like foliage.
²⁹ He who troubles his own house will
inherit the wind,
And the fool will be servant to the wise of heart.

³⁰ The fruit of the righteous is a tree of life,
And he who wins souls is wise.
³¹ If the righteous will be recompensed
on the earth,
How much more the ungodly and the sinner.

In the Chapter
Righteousness (a gift of God) vs. Wickedness (an assault of Satan)
Much of Proverbs is an antithetical list of "ifs" and "buts." If we do this . . . we will be rewarded, but if we do this . . . we will suffer accordingly. Chapter eleven continues this contrast, providing descriptions and the consequences of the righteous versus the wicked, or the opposite sides of a coin, where one side represents good, and the other side represents evil. One side is of God, the other of Satan.

Using words like righteous, gracious, integrity, and merciful; and wickedness, dishonest, evil, and ungodly; I believe this chapter speaks about the spiritual heart of man, and not simply the physical mind or conscience. It deals with our inward intent, or rather the source of our intent. If our hearts are righteous, we will be guided and have the ability to do good things, and we, and those around us, will reap benefits. But if our hearts are full of deception, we, and those around us, will suffer.

This is really the meat of the whole book of Proverbs. If we allow God to live within us and make our hearts righteous, we are able to accomplish righteous actions and results. But if we attempt to do good deeds in and of our self-limiting physical selves, or as a result of allowing Satan to rule our lives, we will fail—today and in the judgment.

In addition to using the words *spirit* and *heart* in this chapter (in contrast to using the words *mind* and *conscience*), the original text also uses the words *soul* or *souls* (in contrast to using the words *body* or *bodies*) in two places— Proverbs 11:17 and 11:30—and I believe this is significant.

"The merciful man does good for [or to] his own soul," and "He who wins souls is wise" (or wise men win souls). I believe Solomon is using language to persuade the reader to think on a more sub-conscious or un-conscious level. Showing mercy not only benefits our physical existence, but, more importantly, our soul. God supplies us with the gift of mercy and the gift to be merciful to others, and by utilizing this gift, we nourish our soul. As we nourish our soul, we become even more equipped to supply this gift and other Godly gifts to those around us. And as we offer our Godly derived gifts to mankind, we win souls for God, and they are provided the same gifts as ourselves.

In Our Homes
Stimulating a Righteous Response
In chapter eleven, Solomon is not talking about emotional reactions, but qualities of being. In order for us to exhibit righteousness to our families, we must allow God to live within our hearts and souls. Much too often we as fathers, mothers, brothers, or sisters act out of emotional response to some negative or positive stimuli. But, God can actually evolve our inward and outward being so that righteous actions become an automatic response to these same stimuli, and with our righteous acts our friends and families are blessed—"When it goes well with the righteous, the city rejoices" (11:10). "By the blessing of the upright the city is exalted" (11:11).

Likewise, if we allow our worldly minds or the counsel of evil to guide our being, we and our families will suffer. "He who troubles his own house will inherit the wind" (11:29). "And there is one who withholds more than is right, but it leads to poverty" (11:24).

 hapter 12

Proverbs 12

[1] Whoever loves instruction loves knowledge,
But he who hates correction is stupid.
[2] A good man obtains favor from the LORD,
But a man of wicked intentions
He will condemn.
[3] A man is not established by wickedness,
But the root of the righteous cannot be moved.
[4] An excellent wife is the crown of her husband,
But she who causes shame
is like rottenness in his bones.
[5] The thoughts of the righteous are right,
But the counsels of the wicked are deceitful.
[6] The words of the wicked are,
"Lie in wait for blood,"
But the mouth of the
upright will deliver them.
[7] The wicked are overthrown and are no more,
But the house of the righteous will stand.
[8] A man will be commended
according to his wisdom,
But he who is of a perverse
heart will be despised.
[9] Better is the one who is slighted
but has a servant,
Than he who honors himself but lacks bread.
[10] A righteous man regards the life of his animal,
But the tender mercies of the wicked are cruel.
[11] He who tills his land will
be satisfied with bread,
But he who follows frivolity
is devoid of understanding.
[12] The wicked covet the catch of evil men,
But the root of the righteous yields fruit.
[13] The wicked is ensnared by the
transgression of his lips,
But the righteous will
come through trouble.
[14] A man will be satisfied
with good by the fruit of his mouth,
And the recompense of a man's

hands will berendered to him.
15 The way of a fool is right in his own eyes,
But he who heeds counsel is wise.
16 A fool's wrath is known at once,
But a prudent man covers shame.
17 He who speaks truth
declares righteousness,
But a false witness, deceit.
18 There is one who speaks like
the piercings of a sword,
But the tongue of the wise promotes health.
19 The truthful lip shall be established forever,
But a lying tongue is but for a moment.
20 Deceit is in the heart of those who devise evil,
But counselors of peace have joy.
21 No grave trouble will overtake the righteous,
But the wicked shall be filled with evil.
22 Lying lips are an abomination to the LORD,
But those who deal truthfully are His delight.
23 A prudent man conceals knowledge,
But the heart of fools proclaims foolishness.
24 The hand of the diligent will rule,
But the lazy man will be put to forced labor.
25 Anxiety in the heart of man causes depression,
But a good word makes it glad.
26 The righteous should choose
his friends carefully,
For the way of the
wicked leads them astray.
27 The lazy man does not roast
what he took in hunting,
But diligence is man's
precious possession.
28 In the way of righteousness is life,
And in its pathway there is no death.

In the Chapter
The Opposite Paths
Chapter twelve continues with its list of opposites and the consequences of living on one side or the other—following good or following evil. If we share good words; seek Godly counsel; follow after righteousness and peace; do honest work for our living; speak the truth; and choose our friends wisely, we are told that blessings of health, physical reward, joy, peace, and life will follow (12: 5,

18, 19, 22, 24, 26, 27, 28). If we follow after foolishness; wicked deeds; or shameful, perverted, and frivolous activity, we will be filled with evil; will often do without the things we need like food and good things; will be overthrown in our pursuits; suffer poor health; and will receive death as our punishment.

Excellence and a Crown
One verse particularly stands out to me as different from the rest of this chapter. Proverbs 12:4 states that "an excellent wife is the crown of her husband."

If we use the text of chapter eleven and twelve to define excellence, then an excellent wife is a Godly wife who is humble, is upright, has integrity, is faithful, grows in knowledge, is wise, seeks after Godly counsel, is gracious and with honor, is discrete, is generous, seeks after good, loves instruction, speaks positive words, is not lazy but works with her hands and her heart, speaks truth, is prudent (wise in the ways of practical affairs), and selects good friends to be her mentors and to whom she can be a good mentor.

When I think of a crown, I think of an ornamental covering for the head made of special metals and precious jewels. And when worn, it signifies power, authority, achievement, dignity, honor, and sovereignty over a geographical area, but also a sign of significant responsibility. I think of a king or a queen of ancient time, when they indeed did rule and were not merely holding a position of prestige.

In Our Homes
Husband and Wife
We cannot incorrectly suppose that these above qualities of human existence are available without God's intervention into our lives, actually into our very souls, or that these qualities of existence are meant only to define an excellent wife. For the words *man*, *him*, and *he* are used more often than the word *she* in these chapters. These scriptures are stating that "whoever . . ." (Proverbs 12:1), man or woman, is to follow after righteousness, but that when a married woman does so, she becomes the crown (the precious mental

and jewels that represents the honor, dignity, sovereignty, and responsibility) of her husband. A righteous wife has the respect of her husband, the adoration of her husband, and represents not only herself out in public and with her family, but represents her husband as well. They are seen as one in the way they present themselves to the world and to God. The one who wears the crown, who is the crown (the wife), shares in the responsibilities and the rewards.

A crown is something of extreme value. A king is going to make sure his crown is cared for, that it is appropriately adorned, and that it receives honor and respect. The crown is a gift from his kingdom. A king would never hit or throw his crown; he would never speak disrespectfully of his crown, not in private or in public; he would always wear it with pride and dignity; and he would care for it as if it were an extension of himself. A husband "first" has the responsibility to do these things for his wife—to treat her with respect and honor, both with his words and his actions.

A good wife is a gift from God's kingdom. The wife, in turn, has the responsibility to be a crown of righteousness and not of shame in the way she treats and speaks of her husband. A good husband is a gift from God's kingdom as well. When a couple takes these concepts of commitment, respect, honor, and love to heart they will find a life of bliss. Not a bliss defined as everything always going my way, or perfect health, or excessive happiness (which can all be taken away), but a bliss of completeness, security, trust, respect, commitment, and foundational love—an I am okay, even when facing turmoil, kind of bliss.

"Hope deferred makes the heart sick,
But when the desire comes, it is a tree of life" (13:12).

 hapter 13

Proverbs 13

[1] A wise son heeds his father's instruction,
But a scoffer does not listen to rebuke.
[2] A man shall eat well by the
fruit of his mouth,
But the soul of the
unfaithful feeds on violence.
[3] He who guards his mouth
preserves his life,
But he who opens wide his
lips shall have destruction.
[4] The soul of a lazy man
desires, and has nothing;
But the soul of the diligent s
hall be made rich.
[5] A righteous man hates lying,
But a wicked man is loathsome
and comes to shame.
[6] Righteousness guards him
whose way is blameless,
But wickedness overthrows
the sinner.
[7] There is one who makes
himself rich, yet has nothing;
And one who makes himself
poor, yet has great riches.
[8] The ransom of a man's life is his riches,
But the poor does not hear rebuke.
[9] The light of the righteous rejoices,
But the lamp of the wicked will be put out.
[10] By pride comes nothing but strife,
But with the well-advised is wisdom.
[11] Wealth gained by dishonesty will
be diminished,
But he who gathers by labor will increase.
[12] Hope deferred makes the heart sick,
But when the desire comes, it is a tree of life.
[13] He who despises the word will be destroyed,
But he who fears the commandment
will be rewarded.
[14] The law of the wise is a fountain of life,

To turn one away from the snares of death.
¹⁵ Good understanding gains favor,
But the way of the unfaithful is hard.
¹⁶ Every prudent man acts with knowledge,
But a fool lays open his folly.
¹⁷ A wicked messenger falls into trouble,
But a faithful ambassador brings health.
¹⁸ Poverty and shame will come to him
who disdains correction,
But he who regards a
rebuke will be honored.
¹⁹ A desire accomplished is
sweet to the soul,
But it is an abomination
to fools to depart from evil.
²⁰ He who walks with wise
men will be wise,
But the companion of
fools will be destroyed.
²¹ Evil pursues sinners,
But to the righteous,
good shall be repaid.
²² A good man leaves an
inheritance to his children's children,
But the wealth of the sinner is
stored up for the righteous.
²³ Much food is in the fallow ground of the poor,
And for lack of justice there is waste.
²⁴ He who spares his rod hates his son,
But he who loves him disciplines
him promptly.
²⁵ The righteous eats to the
satisfying of his soul,
But the stomach of the
wicked shall be in want.

△ △ △

In the Chapter

For chapter thirteen of Proverbs, I would like to address three major topics: the sacred aspect of the written and spoken word, the concept of rich versus poor, and a Biblical appreciation for appropriate desire.

What We Say

The chapter begins with how a son should regard his father's directives—"a wise son heeds his father's instruction" (Proverbs 13:1). It continues with these views about words, whether written or spoken: the fruit of our mouth (our upright words) will affect our ability to eat well (13:2); when we guard our words (take care in the selection and use of our words), we preserve or protect our lives from evil and harm (13:3); if we are righteous (made so by the grace of God and the Spirit of God living within our soul, and not by our own good deeds), we will not feel the need to lie and will, indeed, have the ability to refrain from lying (13:5); and when we are "faithful ambassadors" (when we share good words with others), we avoid trouble, poverty, and shame and find that we are gifted with a quality of good health (13:17).

Rich in Spirit
A second topic for thought is the impression of riches vs. a state of impoverishment. "There is one who makes himself rich, yet has nothing; and there is one who makes himself poor, yet has great riches" (Proverbs 13:7). This verse speaks of the inability of the tangible qualities of life to make one rich in spirit, and a need to, at some level, devoid our dependence on tangible things in order to obtain the riches offered by the spiritual.

Now, to complicate matters, other verses in Proverbs also state the ability of the intangible quality of a spiritual life to bring about tangible blessings. What are the combined implications of these various statements from the Proverbs on rich vs. poor for us as physical human beings?

While our physical life depends on a level of attention to physical things (physical riches), our spiritual life has no dependence on these things. Our spiritual riches may bring about some physical riches, but without any definitive promise of such. In fact, an intended decision not to build our life around physical riches may bring about more spiritual blessings. While these verses do not instruct us to force ourselves to become poor in order to obtain spiritual blessings, they do guide us to heed Godly instruction about the dangers of becoming entangled in the web that physical riches may bring. I love one of the last verses which notes, "A good man leaves an inheritance to his children's children" (13:22). From the other parts of this chapter, I believe it is implied that this inheritance is a passing on of spiritual principals and spiritual blessings.

The Direction of Desire
The final topic for my discussion within this chapter is the idea of there being a Godly appreciation for appropriate desire in mankind. "Hope deferred makes the heart sick, but when the desire comes, it is a tree of life" (Proverbs 13:12). Desire is a God-given gift to be appreciated and experienced, but it is also to be mastered by our spirit controlled by the Spirit of God living within us. Hope is built on desire and faith. We believe something, we desire it, we hope for it, and we create an avenue to move toward it. If our hope and desire is for spiritual growth and development for ourselves, our loved ones, society, humanity, and the environment, it brings about unlimited blessings, some of which are physical, and all of which are spiritual.

In Our Homes
Sacred Words
The principal of the sacred aspect of words begins with the Godly directives of our parents, which often come from the Godly directive of their parents. But if we are not blessed with Godly parents and grandparents, it begins with us. These words can be spoken through letters, cards, notes, emails, phone calls, and most importantly through personal contact—family time together. They can be congratulations, encouragement, or compliments. Our words, and the words of those before us and after us, will have a dramatic effect on those that follow. We need to bless our children and our children's children with our words. Several years ago I began to write and publish books. One of the major reasons I do so is to leave a piece of myself behind for others to encounter. I hope my children and my children's children will read my journals and my books and in so doing get to know me through my words.

Words will build or destroy a home. We must learn to guard our words, to heed Godly instruction, to avoid the snare of lying, and to share good words with others, every day. If we have positive thoughts we should be more apt to share them often, and when we have negative thoughts, we should place a sentinel between them and our mouth in order to safeguard those we might expose to our unconstructive warfare of words. Through the words we use with our family, every day, we can show them respect and support and instill confidence and a sense of authentic security.

Rich vs. Poor
In our homes, we are often more concerned with providing physical benefits to our family over spiritual ones. While parents are called by God to care for the needs of our children, and spouses receive the same calling to care for the needs of each other, we must work harder to better understand the holistic ramifications of placing the physical above the spiritual when it comes to riches. If we as grandparents, parents, children, and siblings will begin to do everything we do under a spiritual umbrella from which hang the concepts of shelter, food, clothing, and security, we build a solid foundation around these physical benefits. Our physical needs should be based on spiritual principals. If we use our physical blessings to expand the stretch of God to our families and the world outside our families, we, and our world, will be blessed.

My family has enjoyed times of physical richness and times when we were physically poor, but the one think I noted was that during both times, we had most of the same things (a home, food, clothing, a car). Now I will admit that during times of richness, these things were of greater physical quality, but at the level of need, they were the same. Within this country, I believe that if we are willing to go out and make a living, with wisdom we can live on what we make.

Godly Desires
We should create Godly desires for every aspect of our lives. I firmly believe that we can do all things that are required for our physical existence through and by the Spirit of God. We are most limited by our own physical self-inflected restraints. As we serve our family, we can do every-

thing for a greater good, not for what we may get in return. We can do everything with purpose and a desire for good, rather than for simple physical reward and reciprocation.

Spouses, enjoy the desire for sexual pleasure, yet be true to this desire with your committed, life partner. Parents, enjoy the desire to spend time with your children, and grandparents to spend time with your children and grandchildren, but do it with a concern for their wellbeing above your own, putting their immediate family (your children and their children) first. We must honor our parents, but we must also honor our children in their role of becoming parents to their children. Respect their wishes. Desire good things for your family, hope for these good things, and go after them, but utilize the gift of God's Spirit in prioritizing and accomplishing this task, and more blessings will flow. "A desire accomplished is sweet to the soul" (Proverbs 13:19).

 hapter 14

Proverbs 14

¹ The wise woman builds her house,
  But the foolish pulls it down
  with her hands.
² He who walks in his uprightness
  fears the LORD,
  But he who is perverse in
  his ways despises Him.
³ In the mouth of a fool is a rod of pride,
  But the lips of the wise will preserve them.
⁴ Where no oxen are, the trough is clean;
  But much increase comes by the
  strength of an ox.
⁵ A faithful witness does not lie,
  But a false witness will utter lies.
⁶ A scoffer seeks wisdom and
  does not find it,
  But knowledge is easy to
  him who understands.
⁷ Go from the presence of
  a foolish man,
  When you do not perceive
  in him the lips of knowledge.
⁸ The wisdom of the prudent is to
  understand his way,
  But the folly of fools is deceit.
⁹ Fools mock at sin,
  But among the upright there is favor.
¹⁰ The heart knows its own bitterness,
  And a stranger does not share its joy.
¹¹ The house of the wicked will be overthrown,
  But the tent of the upright will flourish.
¹² There is a way that seems right to a man,
  But its end is the way of death.
¹³ Even in laughter the heart may sorrow,
  And the end of mirth may be grief.
¹⁴ The backslider in heart will be filled
  with his own ways,
  But a good man will be satisfied from above.
¹⁵ The simple believes every word,
  But the prudent considers well his steps.

¹⁶ A wise man fears and departs from evil,
   But a fool rages and is self-confident.
¹⁷ A quick-tempered man acts foolishly,
   And a man of wicked intentions is hated.
¹⁸ The simple inherit folly,
   But the prudent are
   crowned with knowledge.
¹⁹ The evil will bow before the good,
   And the wicked at the gates
   of the righteous.
²⁰ The poor man is hated even
   by his own neighbor,
   But the rich has many friends.
²¹ He who despises his neighbor sins;
   But he who has mercy on the poor,
   happy is he.
²² Do they not go astray who devise evil?
   But mercy and truth belong to those who
   devise good.
²³ In all labor there is profit,
   But idle chatter leads only to poverty.
²⁴ The crown of the wise is their riches,
   But the foolishness of fools is folly.
²⁵ A true witness delivers souls,
   But a deceitful witness speaks lies.
²⁶ In the fear of the LORD there is
   strong confidence,
   And His children will have a place of refuge.
²⁷ The fear of the LORD is a fountain of life,
   To turn one away from the snares of death.
²⁸ In a multitude of people is a king's honor,
   But in the lack of people is the downfall
   of a prince.
²⁹ He who is slow to wrath
   has great understanding,
   But he who is impulsive exalts folly.
³⁰ A sound heart is life to the body,
   But envy is rottenness to the bones.
³¹ He who oppresses the poor
   reproaches his Maker,
   But he who honors Him
   has mercy on the needy.
³² The wicked is banished in his wickedness,
   But the righteous has a refuge in his death.
³³ Wisdom rests in the heart of him who
   has understanding,
   But what is in the heart
   of fools is made known.
³⁴ Righteousness exalts a nation,

But sin is a reproach to any people.
35 The king's favor is toward a wise servant,
But his wrath is against him who causes shame.

In the Chapter

Four topics stand out to me in Proverbs 14: the wise and the foolish, the effects of lying, prudent living, and following that which seems right and okay but is not.

The Wise and the Foolish

I think most of the Proverbs touch on the concepts of wise and foolish thinking and action, and chapter fourteen is no exception. The wise build up, and the foolish tear down (14:1). The fool will falter from his pride, but the wise will preserve (14:3). Man should flee from the presence of one who is foolish (14:7). Fools are full of deceit and make fun of the concept of sin (14:8–9). The wise fear (respect) the power of evil, but the fool is overly confident in his egotistical abilities (14:16). And the ways of a foolish heart will be "made known" with recompense, while the heart of the wise will be revealed and find favor (14:33–35).

Lying

Proverbs 14:5 and 25 state that "a faithful witness does not lie," and "a deceitful witness speaks lies." As humans we will be called to witness at many times and in many ways. We will become know as men and women of our word, or as deceitful, self-centered liars. It only takes one lie to be a false witness, and it takes being caught in a lie only once to ruin our reputation and those we bare witness against.

Prudency

Prudent is a word we do not use today, maybe because we associate it with that which is boring or typical. But in verses eight and sixteen the word prudent is associated with Godly wisdom. It is a careful and cautious examination of that which is laid before us. A prudent man or woman has the ability to distinguish between folly and intellectual insight. Prudency does not imply an automatic degree of boredom and lack of creativity. It simply implies that we examine something before we react or respond, and we think and act with a balance of intellectual/analytically review and creative/experiential exploration. We act from both the head and the heart. We can be a prudent free-spirit just as much as we can be a folly-full free-spirit, but to do so we must be able to differentiate between foolish advice and wise counsel. Follow after that which enchants you, but with a prudent eye and cautious steps.

That Which Seems Right, but is Not
The final verse for my thoughts is Proverbs 14:12, because it catches all of us off guard at times: "There is a way that seems right to man, but its end is the way of death." I call this the one spirit short principle. We can act from our heart and spirit, and that call may be initiated by the Spirit of God, but it may be our heart and spirit being led by our flesh. Since man has a spirit, we can be "spiritual" beings and only follow after our own spirit. But, if we are to be authentic in our spirituality, we must assure that we examine where our spiritual guidance originates. Perhaps we are one spirit short and are simply following after our own spirit, which may, or may not, be guided by God. We must get to know our own heart and spirit intimately, and be able to discriminate between a true spiritual calling and a pseudo calling.

In Our Homes
The Wise and the Foolish
The lesson for the home from this section is that our foolish ways will find us out, and our family will suffer. Pride and egotism have no place in the management of a family. Rather, we should follow after Godliness and the guidance of wise mentors. Our role as parents is to be upright in our thoughts and action; to allow or children to see us as wise in our decision making, leading them to desire to follow after what it is they see in us.

Lying
My children were taught to be honest even when it meant they would pay the consequences imme-

diately, because, you see, there are consequences, or results, both ways (consequences for lying and consequences for telling the truth). The difference is that the consequences for telling the truth bear good along with any pain, but the consequences for lying carry no genuine positive outcomes. We might get out of something temporarily, but our lies will find us out at some point. Lying, builds on lying, builds on lying—then it topples. Truth, builds on truth, builds on truth—and it stands firm.

Children will follow what that see in their parents. If white lies are okay with us, they will tell even greater white lies; if open lying is okay with us, they will drown in lies. May our children never catch us in a lie, not because we are sly in our ability to lie, but because we will not allow ourselves to tell a lie.

A recommendation I often share is that when confronting people you believe have lied, do not put them in a corner without giving them time to think through the consequences of lying and the consequences of telling the truth. When we do not have time to think, our physical, survivalist instincts will take over to preserve what we believe to be our well-being. I prefer to confront people who may have lied and allow them time to get back with me, rather than answer me immediately.

Prudency
I am what I like to call a prudent free-spirit. I love mystery, enchantment, and creative and experiential learning, but I want it to be shored up by a balance of academic, intellectual, and analytical support. I do not accept someone's words as truth simply because he speaks intellectually or creatively about a topic of interest to me, and I do not seek enchantment through folly.

I believe children are the most likely of humans to see beyond the physical into the spiritual world of enchantment and mystery, and sometimes this pursuit can encourage them to follow after folly, which scares parents. So what do we do?

As we train our children to become adults, we

tend to mind-muscle this sense of awe out of them as a trait that is much too fanciful for an adult. We stop them from tasting crayons, from catching fireflies, and they become prudent bores. My advice for this section may seem strange, but I want to encourage parents to create prudent free-spirits—children who grow into adults with a continued sense of fascination with our world.

A prudent fascination is one that allows us to carefully examine what is around us every day and takes worthwhile risks. It encourages us to be cautious in trying new things, yet willing to do so. It teaches us to be discreet in the way we present ourselves, yet have a willingness to be ourselves through individual expression. And it has a practical side supported by a sense of romance. A prudent free-spirit is one who balances the intellectual with the creative and finds joy in the life he lives.

That Which Seems Right, but is Not
This may be the hardest of the four topics I have discussed in guiding our family to follow. We tend to think that when we believe that we are right, we are indeed right. The problem is six fold:
1) Sometimes there is more than one right answer. (We might be right, and our spouse or children may also be right, yet our beliefs seem in opposition.)
2) Sometimes we believe that we are right, and we, plain and simply, are not. (We are just stubborn.)
3) Sometimes there is so much confusion in our pathway that it is very difficult to distinguish right from wrong.
4) Sometimes we are following after our physical mind and it's self-preserving desires, which make it appear right while it may not be.
5) Sometimes we are following after our spirit, but our spirit is not in tune with the Spirit of God.
6) And last but not least, far too seldom are we following after our spirit in direct harmony with God's Spirit.

The real key to this complicated phenomenon is to set our desires on Christ in all things. It requires that our spirit, our soul, our mind, and our body approach everything we do as spiritual, and that we allow God to be our Spirit-Guide. If we can learn to change a diaper as a spiritual duty, to make love as a spiritual gift, to wash dishes as a spiritual task, and to work and make a financial living as a spiritual vocation, the confusion dissipates, and at some point we, plain and simply, begin to do good things and right things because they become the way we are re-encoded.

# Chapter 15

Proverbs 15

1 A soft answer turns away wrath,
   But a harsh word stirs up anger.
2 The tongue of the wise uses knowledge rightly,
   But the mouth of fools pours forth foolishness.
3 The eyes of the LORD are in every place,
   Keeping watch on the evil and the good.
4 A wholesome tongue is a tree of life,
   But perverseness in it breaks the spirit.
5 A fool despises his father's instruction,
   But he who receives correction is prudent.
6 In the house of the righteous
   there is much treasure,
   But in the revenue of the
   wicked is trouble.
7 The lips of the wise disperse knowledge,
   But the heart of the fool does not do so.
8 The sacrifice of the wicked is an
   abomination to the LORD,
   But the prayer of the
   upright is His delight.
9 The way of the wicked is an
   abomination to the LORD,
   But He loves him who
   follows righteousness.
10 Harsh discipline is for him
   who forsakes the way,
   And he who hates
   correction will die.
11 Hell and Destruction are
   before the LORD;
   So how much more the
   hearts of the sons of men.
12 A scoffer does not love
   one who corrects him,
   Nor will he go to the wise.
13 A merry heart makes a cheerful countenance,
   But by sorrow of the heart the spirit is broken.
14 The heart of him who has understanding
   seeks knowledge,
   But the mouth of fools feeds on foolishness.

¹⁵ All the days of the afflicted are evil,
But he who is of a merry heart has a continual feast.
¹⁶ Better is a little with the fear of the LORD,
Than great treasure with trouble.
¹⁷ Better is a dinner of herbs where love is,
Than a fatted calf with hatred.
¹⁸ A wrathful man stirs up strife,
But he who is slow to anger allays contention.
¹⁹ The way of the lazy man is like a hedge of thorns,
But the way of the upright is a highway.
²⁰ A wise son makes a father glad,
But a foolish man despises his mother.
²¹ Folly is joy to him who is destitute of discernment,
But a man of understanding walks uprightly.
²² Without counsel, plans go awry,
But in the multitude of counselors they are established.
²³ A man has joy by the answer of his mouth,
And a word spoken in due season, how good it is!
²⁴ The way of life winds upward for the wise,
That he may turn away from hell below.
²⁵ The LORD will destroy the house of the proud,
But He will establish the boundary of the widow.
²⁶ The thoughts of the wicked are an abomination to the LORD,
But the words of the pure are pleasant.
²⁷ He who is greedy for gain troubles his own house,
But he who hates bribes will live.
²⁸ The heart of the righteous studies how to answer,
But the mouth of the wicked pours forth evil.

29 The LORD is far from the wicked,
But He hears the prayer of the righteous.
30 The light of the eyes rejoices the heart,
And a good report makes the bones healthy.
31 The ear that hears the rebukes of life
Will abide among the wise.
32 He who disdains instruction
despises his own soul,
But he who heeds rebuke
gets understanding.
33 The fear of the LORD is
the instruction of wisdom,
And before honor is humility.

In the Chapter
Proverbs 15 once again speaks of the power of words and adds a new topic—A Merry Heart.

Soft Words vs. Harsh Words
This chapter begins by directing us as men and women to be careful in the selection of our words and how we speak these words: "A soft answer turns away wrath, but a harsh word stirs up anger" (Proverbs 15:1). The chapter continues by noting the use of foolish words versus a "wholesome tongue" (15:2, 4), the sharing of wisdom through the words that come from our lips (15:7), spreading joy and good tidings through our words (15:23), and selecting the right words for the right occasion (15:23, 26).

Our choice of words, the inflection of our voices (soft, loud, harsh, kind) when we share our words, and the intent of our spirits when we speak our words, all affect our listeners. Any harsh words we think, and then share, first affect our own spirits and minds. If the thoughts we are about to put into words cause us mental pain and anguish, we must consider if they are the right words to use. If they are coming forth, pushed from behind by anger, we would do well to wait to share them until we have time to mellow our spirits and minds.

Sometimes we need to share painful things through our words, but, even then, the way in which we share them often carries more power than the actual words. This chapter's overall directives are to think through our words before we speak them; to not speak while in the depths of anger; and to not use perverse language, but instead speak with a kind heart and with the knowledge of how our words may affect others.

A Merry Heart
The second topic that deserves our time is the concept of a Merry Heart. "A merry heart makes a cheerful countenance, but by sorrow of the heart the spirit is broken" (Proverbs 15:13). "He who has a merry heart has a continual feast" (15:15). "The heart of the righteous studies how to answer" (15:28).

What is this heart Proverbs speaks of? It is not the biological heart that pumps blood throughout our human body, but it is the spiritual heart; the spirit of our mind; the thinking, feeling, emotional part of our soul. We have a physical mind that thinks and our body responds, and we have a spiritual mind (our spirit) that thinks and our soul responds. We then use our physical mind and body to express our spirit and our soul. The question we must ask ourselves is do our words come from our self-centered physical mind; from our individual spirit, but so directed by our physical mind and body; or from a direct relationship with our God and His Spirit?

The blessings of a cheerful or joyful heart, and the ability to use righteous words that are derived from the heart, come from a relationship with God. Only by allowing our spirit, soul, mind, and body to be directed by God, can we experience this Merry Heart.

In Our Homes
Soft Words vs. Harsh Words
The lesson to be applied in our homes from this chapter is to examine the words we use, and the way we share them with our family members before, we speak them. Are we speaking out of anger, out of selfishness, or out of a lack of appropriate knowledge of the subject matter at hand? If so, we must examine our thoughts before they become our words and often simply remain quiet, or at least wait to speak until we have had the time

to determine the source of our harsh thoughts and words and to create a more positive approach to what we need to share. Often times, we need to determine a way to deliver our words in a more appropriate manner than that for which our automatic response system suggests.

We should praise and compliment our children and our spouses often. We should develop a list of appropriate words of praise as well as appropriate words of reprimand. And we should make a point of building up our family with our words and how we use them. Each member of our family should be made to feel important in our presence. We must learn to channel our words through our hearts and our heart-felt words through the Spirit of God.

A Merry Heart
What a wonder blessing and gift to share in our homes—the gift of a merry heart. A merry heart can be felt and seen in our actions, in our demeanor, in our personality, in our praise, and even in our punishment or correction when needed. A merry heart begins as a gift of God and from God. It is of Him because it is a part of His nature shared with those who follow after Him, and it is a gift from Him, to those who share in His glory as children of God. It can then be shared with others through a holistic and merry spirit, soul, mind, and body.

The term merry, as used here, does not imply continual happiness and outward fun every minute of the day, but rather an inner contentment expressed by a pleasant demeanor—a contentment that exists in times of joy as well as in times of distress. A merry-ness that comes only from our physical characteristics (our physical mind and body) cannot stand firm in times of distress. As parents and spouses, we must allow God to be the source of our merry heart, and we must share this heart each and every day with those around us.

# Chapter 16

Proverbs 16

¹ The preparations of the
   heart belong to man,
   But the answer of the
   tongue is from the LORD.
² All the ways of a man are
   pure in his own eyes,
   But the LORD weighs the spirits.
³ Commit your works to the LORD,
   And your thoughts will be established.
⁴ The LORD has made all for Himself,
   Yes, even the wicked for the day of doom.
⁵ Everyone proud in heart is an
   abomination to the LORD;
   Though they join forces,
   none will go unpunished.
⁶ In mercy and truth
   Atonement is provided for iniquity;
   And by the fear of the LORD one
   departsfrom evil.
⁷ When a man's ways please the LORD,
   He makes even his enemies to be
   at peace with him.
⁸ Better is a little with righteousness,
   Than vast revenues without justice.
⁹ A man's heart plans his way,
   But the LORD directs his steps.
¹⁰ Divination is on the lips of the king;
   His mouth must not transgress in judgment.
¹¹ Honest weights and scales are the LORD's;
   All the weights in the bag are His work.
¹² It is an abomination for kings
   to commit wickedness,
   For a throne is established by righteousness.
¹³ Righteous lips are the delight of kings,
   And they love him who speaks what is right.
¹⁴ As messengers of death is the king's wrath,
   But a wise man will appease it.
¹⁵ In the light of the king's face is life,
   And his favor is like a cloud of the latter rain.
¹⁶ How much better to get wisdom than gold!

And to get understanding is
to be chosen rather than silver.
¹⁷ The highway of the upright is
to depart from evil;
He who keeps his way
preserves his soul.
¹⁸ Pride goes before destruction,
And a haughty spirit before a fall.
¹⁹ Better to be of a humble spirit with the lowly,
Than to divide the spoil with the proud.
²⁰ He who heeds the word wisely will find good,
And whoever trusts in the LORD, happy is he.
²¹ The wise in heart will be called prudent,
And sweetness of the lips increases learning.
²² Understanding is a wellspring of life
to him who has it.
But the correction of fools is folly.
²³ The heart of the wise teaches his mouth,
And adds learning to his lips.
²⁴ Pleasant words are like a honeycomb,
Sweetness to the soul and health to the bones.
²⁵ There is a way that seems right to a man,
But its end is the way of death.
²⁶ The person who labors, labors for himself,
For his hungry mouth drives him on.
²⁷ An ungodly man digs up evil,
And it is on his lips like a burning fire.
²⁸ A perverse man sows strife,
And a whisperer separates the best of friends.
²⁹ A violent man entices his neighbor,
And leads him in a way that is not good.
³⁰ He winks his eye to devise perverse things;
He purses his lips and brings about evil.
³¹ The silver-haired head is a crown of glory,
If it is found in the way of righteousness.
³² He who is slow to anger is
better than the mighty,
And he who rules his spirit
than he who takes a city.
³³ The lot is cast into the lap,
But its every decision is from the LORD.

In the Chapter
The Physical Mind and Conscience versus the Spiritual Mind (the Spirit) and Heart
I would summarize chapter sixteen under the

above title. "All the ways of a man are pure in his eyes, But the Lord weights the spirits" (Proverbs 16:2). We have a tendency to convince ourselves that our ways and thoughts are right and good, and that they are even God-ordained, but we must be careful that this "wise thinking" is indeed wisdom from God, rather than a "physical" level of wisdom.

God sees through our ways, cutting completely through to the spirit and heart. He sees our true motives and desires. He sees our true intent. And this works two ways for the Christian. For as long as we live in our physical bodies, we have both physical and spiritual attributes. When we make bad choices, but have good intent, from a Godly-directed spirit and heart, God knows it, and His saving grace covers over it. "In mercy and truth, atonement is provided for iniquity" (16:6). But, likewise, when we do what appears to be good, but we do it with a contrite heart, God also sees through our façade and will work to re-direct our ways, but we will often still suffer from our misguided self-directives and pay the related consequences. Our difficult task, our challenge as human entities, is to determine the source of our perceived wisdom.

Think of the conscience as the center of the mind and a part of the physical body, and think of the heart as the center of the spirit and a part of our spiritual existence. We can do good things from the mind and conscience, but they are typically for reciprocal benefits, or motivated by fear or inappropriately directed good. Or we can do things from the spirit and heart, directed more toward the appropriate good of humanity, society, or our environment, and not simply for self-benefits. But we can also do things from our spirit and heart that are guided by the world instead of God. We can be "proud in heart" (16:5) and have a "haughty spirit" (16:18), or we can have a "humble spirit" (16:19) and a "wise heart"(16:21). We can allow the world to rule our spirit and heart or we can allow God to rule our spirit and heart. And he who "rules his spirit" (16:32), or more appropriately defined as he who "rules his spirit" under the direct guidance of God as "every decision is from the Lord" (16:33), is blessed far greater than having mere physical power (16:32). And understand this in conclusion: we can only begin to determine whether our perceived wisdom is from God, or from man, by spending enough time with God to discern His voice from that of man and the world in which we live.

In Our Homes
The Physical Mind and Conscience versus the Spiritual Mind (the Spirit) and Heart

In applying this concept to our responsibilities as a member of a household—a father, mother, child, etc.—it seems clear that the advantages of allowing ourselves to be guided by a spirit and heart, which are directed by God, provide immense divine benefits as well as physical, while the benefits of following after our own physical mind and conscience offer mere temporal gains.

If, we, as men, women, or children, can learn to do everything we do spiritually (guided by our spirit and soul which are set upon God and guided by His Spirit), our homes would become places of great comfort, security, respect, and a source of the deepest and highest level of love that can be known. As stated before, with this mindset, or spiritset, we can begin to do everything spiritually from changing a baby's diaper, to cleaning the house, to making love to our spouse. It is about the motive behind, and source of, our action; whom is it for; and where it comes from. If it is about the benefit of others and its source is God, we begin to find a bliss that is unfortunately unknown in most homes.

From the Marriage and Family class I teach at O'More College of Design, I recently conducted a study on the various types of love we may experience inside and outside our homes, and I easily gathered together twenty-eight forms that I have personally experiences over my lifetime—you are likely to gather more.

The four most commonly discussed forms of love come from the Greek and relate to these types of love: a friendship love, a sensual or sexual love, a natural love, and an unconditional love. But what about a love we develop for a caretaker, or them for us; a chemical or animal attraction to someone; a sensual love for one's beauty (inner or outer), but without sexual implications; a spiritual love for one's well-being even if we do not like him; tough love where we do something for one's benefit that is very hard, emotionally, for us to do; a submissive love to a person of authority or a loving spouse; a sacrificial love where you give greatly of yourself; a romantic love, joy in doing for another as a friend or as a lover; a sympathetic love, a feeling of loving sadness for someone's circumstance; an I-want-to-rescue-you-love, the knight in shining armor love; the love we might have for a mentor, one we respect as wise; a dependency or co-dependency love (though these are not so good, because they are often mistaken as a type of real love); a charismatic love for someone's personality; an emotional love, more about what someone can do for you or how he can make you feel; an infatuation love; and etc., etc., etc.

And this list doesn't even begin to note the love we might have for a pet, a type of food, a piece of furniture, our car, our house, our money, our job, nature, art, photography, and etc., etc., etc. Are all these loves directed by God, are they directed by the heart and spirit, are they directed by the physical appetite? Can we experience them and remain faithful to a spouse, or our family? Can we experience them and remain sane? And what about this thing called "unconditional love?" That one seems really troublesome.

The simple answer is that I believe there are basically three types of love— Physical Love, Spiritual Love—Level One, and Spiritual Love—Level Two.

Physical Love encompasses many of the twenty-eight forms of love I noted above and is much like the term happy versus joy. Happy is determined each day by our circumstances, much like various forms of physical love. Joy is something that is a gift of God and allows us to "be okay" even in the midst of turmoil, because of an inner comfort, more like real, true, foundational love— Spiritual Love—Level Two.

Spiritual Love—Level One is generated by our spirit and soul but without the wisdom and guidance of God and His Spirit. While this love is from the heart and carries emotional as well as analytical conceptualization as it foundation, it may be self-centered and directed by the effect of the world on our spirit and soul. I call this "one-Spirit-short spirituality." It is spiritual love because it comes for our spirit, but it is not foundational love as in Spiritual Love—Level Two.

Spiritual Love—Level Two is generated by our spirit and soul but is directed by the Spirit of God as He acts upon us. I believe it is the Only Love that can be truly unconditional, because it is the only love that is granted to man as a Gift of God and from God to share with others. If I am unconditionally to love my wife, my child, my parents, my friends, or others, I must allow it to happen as a gift directly from the nature of God. I cannot do it within myself. Therefore, the types of love I share within my home are many. But, the only way to offer them as unconditional is to place them all under the direct guidance of our spirit and soul guided by the Spirit of God.

In our homes, love can be experienced and expressed in many, many ways. If we can learn to allow our spirit and soul to direct these ways, so-governed by the Spirit of God, we can create a home environment that exceeds all our expectations. And if we can understand the appropriate places for each type of love, and which forms do not belong in our lives, we can avoid the mishaps that so often befall the misguided relationships men and women often develop in an attempt to experience and feel the bliss of being in love.

 hapter 17

Proverbs 17

¹ Better is a dry morsel with quietness,
  Than a house full of feasting with strife.
² A wise servant will rule over
  a son who causes shame,
  And will share an inheritance
  among the brothers.
³ The refining pot is for
  silver and the furnace for gold,
  But the LORD tests the hearts.
⁴ An evildoer gives heed to false lips;
  A liar listens eagerly to
  a spiteful tongue.
⁵ He who mocks the poor
  reproaches his Maker;
  He who is glad at calamity
  will not go unpunished.
⁶ Children's children are the
  crown of old men,
  And the glory of
  children is their father.
⁷ Excellent speech is not
  becoming to a fool,
  Much less lying lips to a prince.
⁸ A present is a precious stone in
  the eyes of its possessor;
  Wherever he turns, he prospers.
⁹ He who covers a transgression seeks love,
  But he who repeats a matter separates friends.
¹⁰ Rebuke is more effective for a wise man
  Than a hundred blows on a fool.
¹¹ An evil man seeks only rebellion;
  Therefore a cruel messenger will
  be sent against him.
¹² Let a man meet a bear
  robbed of her cubs,
  Rather than a fool in his folly.
¹³ Whoever rewards evil for good,
  Evil will not depart from his house.
¹⁴ The beginning of strife is like releasing water;
  Therefore stop contention before a quarrel starts.

¹⁵ He who justifies the wicked,
   and he who condemns the just,
   Both of them alike are an
   abomination to the LORD.
¹⁶ Why is there in the hand of a
   fool the purchase price of wisdom,
   Since he has no heart for it?
¹⁷ A friend loves at all times,
   And a brother is born for adversity.
¹⁸ A man devoid of understanding
   shakes hands in a pledge,
   And becomes surety for his friend.
¹⁹ He who loves transgression loves strife,
   And he who exalts his gate seeks destruction.
²⁰ He who has a deceitful heart finds no good,
   And he who has a perverse
   tongue falls into evil.
²¹ He who begets a scoffer
   does so to his sorrow,
   And the father of a
   fool has no joy.
²² A merry heart does
   good, like medicine,
   But a broken spirit
   dries the bones.
²³ A wicked man accepts
   a bribe behind the back
   To pervert the ways of justice.
²⁴ Wisdom is in the sight of him
   who has understanding,
   But the eyes of a fool are on
   the ends of the earth.
²⁵ A foolish son is a grief to his father,
   And bitterness to her who bore him.
²⁶ Also, to punish the righteous is not good,
   Nor to strike princes for their uprightness.
²⁷ He who has knowledge spares his words,
   And a man of understanding is
   of a calm spirit.
²⁸ Even a fool is counted wise
   when he holds his peace;
   When he shuts his lips, he
   is considered perceptive.

In the Chapter

The two topics that speak to me most from Proverbs 17 are the effects of strife upon a household and the blessing or pain that can be placed upon parents by our children.

The Effects of Strife
Proverbs 17 starts out with a proclamation about the effect of a house filled with strife: "Better is a dry morsel with quietness, than a house full of feasting with strife." Then in verse fourteen Solomon continues: "The beginning of strife is like releasing water; therefore stop contention before a quarrel starts." I have tasted both the boring unseasoned blandness of a dry morsel (old bread) and a feast so full of aromas and textures and flavors, it overwhelmed my senses. I have also experienced the quiet peacefulness of sitting in front of a fireplace, alone or with my wife, reading a great book, as well as the thunderous clatter of a house so full of people and noise that I could not hear myself think. If I had the ability to always select which of these four situations I would prefer, I would select a quiet and peaceful feast. But, like Solomon, if strife must come with the feast, give me bread.

Solomon further offers the comparison of strife with the expansive release of water (17:14). My mind immediately recalls two pictures that visually communicate what Solomon is talking about here. One was the first time I encountered the opening of a great dam and watched as the waters began to plummet uncontrollably (or what seemed to be uncontrollable). The other was the viewing of a river in flood stage washing far beyond it banks, tearing away anything that got in it way—trees, cars, even a building caught up by the waters and wildly battling its way down the middle of what use to be a highway. Solomon says this is a vivid portrait of strife—powerful, wild, uncontrollable, and destructive. His advice? Stop it before it starts.

Within the field of medicine we have learned much about what we now call preventative care or preventative medicine. Over multiple centuries of scientific study, we have learned that there is much more we can do to prevent, or at least reduce, the effects of disease, by our actions, sometimes more so than we can successfully treat disease once we have succumbed to its control. We prevent strife by the same means of prevention—by not creating it ourselves. We prevent strife by working to stop it from ever getting started. We prevent strife by becoming forewarned of its characteristic itinerary and laying a new course to follow. We prevent strife by becoming wise, not wisdom in the ways of the world, but wisdom as given as a gift from God.

Children
Proverbs 17 outlines two very different views of the effect of children on how their family is perceived by the world around them and the emotional mood established in a household relegated by the attitude and behavior of the children within that household.

In verse six, Solomon says that "children's children are the crown of old men, and the glory of children is their father." Then in verse twenty-five, he states, "A foolish son is a grief to his father, and bitterness to her who bore him." If loving, wise, and Spirit-guided, our children and our grandchildren honor and show respect to their parents and grandparents, and those around them will see this honor and respect, and are likely to bestow upon them a similar level of honor and respect. However, an unwise or foolish child is likely to bring heartache and sorrow upon his parents, creating an environment that breeds animosity and hostility for all within that household. While some children may fall away from sound teaching and a loving upbringing, Solomon often speaks of the importance of such teaching and love in creating an environment that nourishes our children and our grandchildren into loving, caring adults.

In Our Homes
The Effects of Strife
In the early days of my now thirty-six-year marriage, I remember countless days of unproductive and unhappy marital strife. Married at nineteen years of age, the male personality and low level of astuteness leaves much to be desired. And even though the female persona runs far ahead of us

male members of society, they, I must say, in their youth, also lack a level of wisdom only provided as a gift of God or from personal experience. Thank God, He has blessed my wife and myself with a significant helping of both—His gifts and life experiences.

In our youth, I don't think that it is so much that we enjoy strife, but we seem to simply be too ignorant to know how to avoid it. We are putter-outers of fires—I speak now of the male species again—but we lack the know-how of how to avoid them. Solomon's wisdom, to be shared with a young couple making a home for themselves today, might be plainly expressed as I was once told by an older gentleman married for over fifty years. "Son, in your marriage, you can either be right, or you can be happy. You pick."

While this is an over simplification and may be perceived as merely faking it to avoid conflict, I regard his advice as one of strife-preventive. I have learned that much of what we tend to fret about, and act stubborn about, in our youth, is simply not important. I have mellowed with age, and I love it. My wife has mellowed with age, and I love it as well. And I would venture to say that she feels the same.

As I write this chapter, I am feeling very playful, and I am sure it will be noted in my writing for Proverbs 17 in comparison with my other nine chapters, which probably take a more serious note, but it is Valentine's Day 2012, and my serious side is taking a day off. In verse twenty-two, Solomon tells us that "a merry heart does good, like medicine." My thoughts for this chapter can be summed up in this verse, and though I've mentioned the merry heart before, I want to look at it in a different way now.

Allow God to give you a merry heart, and share it with someone you love. And do not allow a "broken spirit to dry the bones" (17:22). Allow your soul to come out and play. If you have been married for many years as I have, re-capture the enchantment you once felt in your youth, while using your new-found experiential and God-given wisdom to avoid the pit-falls of youthful strife. And if you are a newly married couple or one contemplating marriage, allow God to give you His gift of wisdom, and remember that you can learn about strife by reading about it from inspired writers, like Solomon, and then lay a course to avoid it, or you can go through the long-suffering pains of personal experiences of strife. I know which I choose today.

Children

I have much to thank God for in my children and my grandchildren who are all a crown upon my head. Should all the wisdom of the world be granted upon me today, I could not have asked for anything more than who my children were in their youth and who they have become as adults. God has blessed me far beyond what I deserve, and I am eternally grateful.

My daughter once told me and my wife— as I recall it was Valentine's Day some twenty years ago—"thank you for not breaking up and ruining my life." There were times when breaking up seemed like a good thing to do. My wife and I have both stated that there were periods in our marriage when we stayed together out of our commitment to God, not to each other. But, we did stay together, and over the years we worked together and made our individual lives, and our life as one, something to be authentically wished for by others. And we are now reaping the rewards of that faithfulness in our children.

I wish to borrow one verse from my daughter's section for this book—Proverbs 22:6—"Train up a child in the way he should go, And when he is old he will not depart from it." I once heard a Bible class teacher share this verse, followed by "of course there are exceptions to every rule." I pray that is not true for this verse, and I pray for all parents to have the God-given ability to so train their children. Thank you God for the great blessing of my children and my grandchildren, and may I never take it for granted.

 hapter 18

Proverbs 18

¹ A man who isolates himself
   seeks his own desire;
   He rages against all wise judgment.
² A fool has no delight in understanding,
   But in expressing his own heart.
³ When the wicked comes, contempt comes also;
   And with dishonor comes reproach.
⁴ The words of a man's mouth are deep waters;
   The wellspring of wisdom is a flowing brook.
⁵ It is not good to show partiality to the wicked,
   Or to overthrow the righteous in judgment.
⁶ A fool's lips enter into contention,
   And his mouth calls for blows.
⁷ A fool's mouth is his destruction,
   And his lips are the snare of his soul.
⁸ The words of a talebearer are like tasty trifles,
   And they go down into the inmost body.
⁹ He who is slothful in his work
   Is a brother to him who is a great destroyer.
¹⁰ The name of the LORD is a strong tower;
   The righteous run to it and are safe.
¹¹ The rich man's wealth is his strong city,
   And like a high wall in his own esteem.
¹² Before destruction the heart
   of a man is haughty,
   And before honor is humility.
¹³ He who answers a matter
   before he hears it,
   It is folly and shame to him.
¹⁴ The spirit of a man will
   sustain him in sickness,
   But who can bear a broken spirit?
¹⁵ The heart of the prudent acquires knowledge,
   And the ear of the wise seeks knowledge.
¹⁶ A man's gift makes room for him,
   And brings him before great men.
¹⁷ The first one to plead his cause seems right,
   Until his neighbor comes and examines him.
¹⁸ Casting lots causes contentions to cease,
   And keeps the mighty apart.

19 A brother offended is harder
to win than a strong city,
And contentions are like
the bars of a castle.
20 A man's stomach shall be
satisfied from the fruit of his mouth;
From the produce of his lips he shall be filled.
21 Death and life are in the power of the tongue,
And those who love it will eat its fruit.
22 He who finds a wife finds a good thing,
And obtains favor from the LORD.
23 The poor man uses entreaties,
But the rich answers roughly.
24 A man who has friends must
himself be friendly,
But there is a friend who
sticks closer than a brother.

In the Chapter

Chapter eighteen deals with two major issues. One is a repetitive topic of many of Proverb's chapters—our words. The other topic is a slight variation on a previous topic relating to the heart, the spirit, and the soul, but it now specifically deals with an impediment I refer to as Soul Wounds or Spirit Wounds. It is on this topic I choose to elaborate.

Soul Wounds
Proverbs 18:14 shares that "the spirit of man will sustain him in sickness, but who can bear a broken spirit?" Based upon earlier discussions from Proverbs on the spiritual heart, the spirit, and the soul, and my personal understanding and earlier argument that these are as real within our human bodies as our cardiovascular system, our physical brain, and our entire physical structure, I wish to define Solomon's words here to mean that within our spirit and our soul, we maintain what is needed to overcome all adversarial conditions that arise in this physical world.

Our spirit has the ability to see us through any sickness that assails us. It does not promise a physical curing from all illness, but a sustainment during such sickness—a spiritual nourishment during times of stress, hardship, and illness—a healing. Perhaps it is at the spiritual level that we first receive this sustainment or healing. And perhaps sometimes we are able to transfer this spiritual action from our spirit, heart, and soul, over into our mind, conscience, and body, while at other times we do not, or cannot. But Solomon adds, if we suffer from a spirit or soul that is broken and wounded, our ability to hold up or move forward, both spiritually and physically, is severely diminished—"But who can bear a broken spirit?" (18:14).

In Our Homes
Soul Wounds at Home
The concept of spirit and soul wounds applies to the home in a variety of ways. It may help here that I first define, in simple terms, the phrase spirit and soul wound.

A spirit or soul wound occurs when, over time, we are attacked at the core of our existence, and our spirit and soul are not shored up by a direct relationship with God to handle the attacks. These wounds begin to appear as the psychological and spiritual residue of our prior actions and experiences—experiences of our own making, but quite often experiences not of our own making, but of that which was done to us. It seems that when physio/spiritual conflict is not resolved in a peaceful manner, under the directives of our maker—God—the result is a wounded spirit or soul. Common signs of soul wounds are unresolved anger, fear, rage, bitter talk, emotional outbursts, shame, withdrawal, depression, suicidal tendencies, resentment, feelings of worthlessness and low self-esteem, lack of commitment, inability to hold a job, alcoholism and other substance abuse, numerous health problems, and acts of physical violence—often within one's own family.

The cause of most soul wounds fits into a category we call abuse—sexual abuse, physical abuse, and prolonged verbal abuse being the major impetus for damage. Unfortunately, much of this abuse actually occurs in what should be the sanctity of the home. The first course of action to avoid soul wounds, and to find healing from soul wounds, is to put on the armor of God. Ephesians 6:12–18 provides the armory for soul wounds, and I encourage you to go there for further support. But, for a summary on this armor—seek after authentic truth, not a movement or earthly leader; from this day forward make right-living a priority and allow God to ultimately make your heart right, understanding you cannot do it without Him; create an inner peace and joy by an active belief in Jesus Christ as the Son of God; place your definitive faith in protection from soul wounds in your Creator, not in M.D.s, Ph.D.s, or counselors (This does not mean you should avoid the assistance of trained professionals, but that they are only meant to assist, not to bring about the fundamental healing of soul wounds.); understand the place of grace and forgiveness as only available as a gift from God for the essential relinquishing of shame and guilt; allow God's Word and God's Spirit to guide your spirit and soul to a place of healing; and pray, not simply with your physical mind, but by connecting your mind with your spirit, and your spirit with the Spirit of God, in asking for strength, guidance, and deliverance. This degree of body armor then becomes not only a protection for the future, but also a means for healing from previous battle wounds.

For a general rule to help you avoid soul wounds in the home, remember that your spouse, your children, your parents, and others you love should always feel important in your presence. If those around you feel that you truly love, appreciate, and respect them, healing can occur, and wounding can be avoided. Our unkind and unsupportive words are often the stinging arrows we hail at others. Pay attention to your words and actions, and if they do not offer an environment of love, support, and respect, ask for God's guidance in overcoming your negative tendencies, then practice, practice, practice putting into play new words and actions of encouragement.

* For more information on this armor and on the subject of soul wounds I refer you to my book: *Spirit-Ritual: Exploring Spirituality Beyond the Sacred Veil.*

 Chapter 19

Proverbs 19

¹ Better is the poor who
 walks in his integrity
 Than one who is perverse
 in his lips, and is a fool.
² Also it is not good for a
 soul to be without knowledge,
 And he sins who hastens with his feet.
³ The foolishness of a man twists his way,
 And his heart frets against the LORD.
⁴ Wealth makes many friends,
 But the poor is separated from his friend.
⁵ A false witness will not go unpunished,
 And he who speaks lies will not escape.
⁶ Many entreat the favor of the nobility,
 And every man is a friend to one
 who gives gifts.
⁷ All the brothers of the
 poor hate him;
 How much more do his
 friends go far from him!
 He may pursue them with
 words, yet they abandon him.
⁸ He who gets wisdom loves his own soul;
 He who keeps understanding will find good.
⁹ A false witness will not go unpunished,
 And he who speaks lies shall perish.
¹⁰ Luxury is not fitting for a fool,
 Much less for a servant to rule
 over princes.
¹¹ The discretion of a man
 makes him slow to anger,
 And his glory is to overlook a transgression.
¹² The king's wrath is like the roaring of a lion,
 But his favor is like dew on the grass.
¹³ A foolish son is the ruin of his father,
 And the contentions of a wife
 are a continual dripping.
¹⁴ Houses and riches are an
 inheritance from fathers,
 But a prudent wife is from the LORD.

¹⁵ Laziness casts one into a deep sleep,
   And an idle person will suffer hunger.
¹⁶ He who keeps the commandment
   keeps his soul,
   But he who is careless
   of his ways will die.
¹⁷ He who has pity on the
   poor lends to the LORD,
   And He will pay back
   what he has given.
¹⁸ Chasten your son
   while there is hope,
   And do not set your
   heart on his destruction.
   For if you rescue him, you
   will have to do it again.
²⁰ Listen to counsel and receive instruction,
   That you may be wise in your latter days.
²¹ There are many plans in a man's heart,
   Nevertheless the LORD's
   counsel—that will stand.
²² What is desired in a man is kindness,
   And a poor man is better than a liar.
²³ The fear of the LORD leads to life,
   And he who has it will abide in satisfaction;
   He will not be visited with evil.
²⁴ A lazy man buries his hand in the bowl,
   And will not so much as bring it to his
   mouth again.
²⁵ Strike a scoffer, and the
   simple will become wary;
   Rebuke one who has understanding,
   and he will discern knowledge.
²⁶ He who mistreats his father and
   chases away his mother
   Is a son who causes shame
   and brings reproach.
²⁷ Cease listening to
   instruction, my son,
   And you will stray from
   the words of knowledge.
²⁸ A disreputable witness
   scorns justice,
   And the mouth of the
   wicked devours iniquity.
²⁹ Judgments are prepared for scoffers,
   And beatings for the backs of fools.

In the Chapter
As I read Proverbs 19, the topic that stood out the most to me was The Benefits of Wealth over Being Poor. And I must admit, I read the chapter three times, always looking for the "but," and I did not find it, at least not in words saying wealth is bad or being poor is good. So I had to re-think this chapter from the other chapters of Proverbs and look for parameters for living and existing with wealth, whereby advantages come, and parameters whereby disadvantages come instead of looking for a verse that says "do this and such will happen, but do this other thing, and this other thing will happen."

The Benefits of Wealth over Being Poor
I will start with the verses about the benefits of wealth versus being poor. "Wealth makes many friends, But the poor is separated from his friends" (19:4). "Many entreat the favor of the nobility. And every man is a friend to one who gives gifts" (19:6). "All the brothers of the poor hate him; How much more do his friends go far from him!" (18:7). "Luxury is not fitting for a fool, Much less for a servant to rule over princes" (19:10). And "houses and riches are an inheritance from fathers" (18:14). Each of these verses states a benefit for having wealth, and none note wealth as a negative quality. So let's begin by stating that wealth, in and of itself, is not only *not* a bad thing, but is a good thing.

Now I will share the parameters framing these verses about the benefits of wealth verses being poor. "He who gets wisdom loves his own soul; He who keeps understanding will find good" (19:8). "He who speaks lies shall perish" (19:9). "The discretion of a man makes him slow to anger, and his glory is to overlook a transgression" (19:11). "Lazyness casts one into a deep sleep, and an idle person will suffer hunger" (19:15). "He who keeps the commandments keeps his soul, but he who is careless of his ways will die" (19:16). "He who has pity on the poor lends to the Lord, and He will pay back what he has given" (19:17). "Listen to counsel and receive instruction, that you may be wise in your latter days (19:20). "There are many plans in a man's heart, nevertheless the Lord's counsel—they will stand" (19:21). "The fear of the Lord leads to life, and he who has it will abide in satisfaction" (19:23). And, "a lazy man buries his hand in the bowl, and will not so much as bring it to his mouth again" (19:24).

Note the words that support the man or woman God is talking about when He speaks of wealth as a benefit: wisdom, understanding, truthfulness—honesty, discretion, slowness to anger, overlooking of transgressions, industriousness, keeper of God's commandments, sympathy, listening to counsel, receiving of instruction, and the fear of the Lord.

The blessings noted as accompanying these attributes are the finding of good; the keeping of one's soul; life, not death; positive pay-back from God; wisdom in your latter days; and an abiding satisfaction.

If the verses about wealth, poverty, positive attributes, and blessings noted in Proverbs 19 are intertwined, this chapter tells us that wealth that is shared and wealth that is accompanied by Godly attributes can bring abundant blessings and benefits to the wealthy and those around them.

In Our Homes

I am been blessed to live life with little, and to live life with much. My family has experienced times when we didn't know how we could pay our bills, and times when we have had much more than was needed to live life comfortably. How then do we know with whom we should share our wealth when and if it comes?

I believe Proverbs, as well other parts of God's Word as presented throughout His scripture, says our first responsibility in sharing our wealth is with our family, then with our friends, then others who God puts before us through our family and friends (including church, work, and our community). Wealth may or may not come to us—it is definitely not a promised commodity. And it may come to us for a time and then leave us. But if it does come, Proverbs 19 tells us the attributes that should accompany it and the blessings that support right living.

Wealth, as noted by Solomon, also brings with it the responsibility of teaching our children how to wisely use the money with which we are blessed. I had my first paying jobs beginning at age eleven and at that time created my first budget. And for the last forty-three years I have lived on a budget and taught my children how to do the same. I have no debt but my home, and my children have done the same. And believe it or not, my grown children have never had credit cards. I know my children will teach their children the same principles about money that I taught them, and I know that in times of wealth and times of poor, my children and my grandchildren will be okay and will always share what they have with their family, their friends, and those God puts before them who need help.

"Bread gained by deceit is sweet to a man,
But afterward his mouth will be filled with gravel" (20:17).

Chapter 20

Proverbs 20

[1] Wine is a mocker,
   Strong drink is a brawler,
   And whoever is led astray
   by it is not wise.
[2] The wrath of a king is like
   the roaring of a lion;
   Whoever provokes him to
   anger sins against his own life.
[3] It is honorable for a man to stop striving,
   Since any fool can start a quarrel.
[4] The lazy man will not plow
   because of winter;
   He will beg during
   harvest and have nothing.
[5] Counsel in the heart of
   man is like deep water,
   But a man of understanding
   will draw it out.
[6] Most men will proclaim
   each his own goodness,
   But who can find a faithful man?
[7] The righteous man walks in
   his integrity;
   His children are
   blessed after him.
[8] A king who sits on the
   throne of judgment
   Scatters all evil with his eyes.
[9] Who can say, "I have made
   my heart clean,
   I am pure from my sin"?
[10] Diverse weights and
   diverse measures,
   They are both alike, an
   abomination to the LORD.
[11] Even a child is known by his deeds,
   Whether what he does is pure and right.
[12] The hearing ear and the seeing eye,
   The LORD has made them both.
[13] Do not love sleep, lest you come to poverty;

Open your eyes, and you
will be satisfied with bread.
14 "It is good for nothing,"
cries the buyer;
But when he has gone
his way, then he boasts.
15 There is gold and a multitude
of rubies,
But the lips of knowledge
are a precious jewel.
16 Take the garment of one who
is surety for a stranger,
And hold it as a pledge
when it is for a seductress.
17 Bread gained by deceit is
sweet to a man,
But afterward his mouth
will be filled with gravel.
18 Plans are established by counsel;
By wise counsel wage war.
19 He who goes about as a
talebearer reveals secrets;
Therefore do not associate with
one who flatters with his lips.
20 Whoever curses his father or his mother,
His lamp will be put out in deep darkness.
21 An inheritance gained hastily at the beginning
Will not be blessed at the end.
22 Do not say, "I will recompense evil;"
Wait for the LORD, and He
will save you.
23 Diverse weights are an
abomination to the LORD,
And dishonest scales are not good.
24 A man's steps are of the LORD;
How then can a man
understand his own way?
25 It is a snare for a man to devote
rashly something as holy,
And afterward to reconsider his vows.
26 A wise king sifts out the wicked,
And brings the threshing wheel over them.
27 The spirit of a man is the lamp of the LORD,
Searching all the inner depths of his heart.
28 Mercy and truth preserve the king,
And by loving kindness
he upholds his throne.
29 The glory of young
men is their strength,

And the splendor of old
men is their gray head.
30 Blows that hurt cleanse away evil,
As do stripes the inner depths of the heart.

In this Chapter
Consequences of Deceit
A flowing theme throughout Proverbs 20 relates to the Consequences of Deceit. The reason for deceitful action usually relates to a perceived advantage to be achieved by such action, but, as Proverbs points out, the consequences are sometimes fatal, and always detrimental. "Diverse weights and diverse measures, they are both alike, an abomination to the Lord" (20:10). "Diverse weights are an abomination to the Lord, and dishonest scales are not good (20:23). "Even a child is known by his deeds, whether what he does is pure and right (20:11).

We can learn deceitful ways at a very early age, and our use of deceit can carry with us into adulthood. We are known by our ways in youth, and we will be known by our ways as adult. If we use deceit, it will find us out. To God, any deceit is scandalous and disgraceful. We tend to place people in two categories, trustworthy and untrustworthy. God's plan for mankind is to become a people of trust, honor, and rightful thoughts and action.

Sometimes we use deceit in what appears to be innocent, good business sense to obtain a bargain. "'It is good for nothing,' cries the buyer; but when he has gone his way, then he boasts" (20:14). This one hits home, because I like to bargain with folks. And while the writer is not telling us it is wrong to bargain, he is telling us it is wrong to be deceitful in our bargaining. If we know something is of great value, and we take advantage of someone willfully for self-gain, that is deceit.

"Bread gained by deceit is sweet to a man, but afterward his mouth will be filled with gravel" (20:17). We can use the excuse that if we need something badly enough that perhaps it is okay to come by it with any means possible, even deceit. But Proverbs 20:17 tells us that the consequences of such are not pleasant. The taking may seem sweet, but the effect upon our person is as unpleasant as taking a handful of dirt and gravel into our mouth.

Another type of deceit is so-called righteous deceit, quite often done on an impulse—as a spontaneous gesture that is not well thought out. Or we sometimes try to make a deal with God that we do not plan to keep, or cannot keep, or we make as a rash decision. We make a vow to do something, or to set aside something for God or for the good of mankind, then we change our mind; we take back our vow and make other plans that better suit our perceived needs. Perhaps our moment of devotion has passed, or our imminent danger has subsided, and what we promised is now retrieved. "It is a snare for a man to devote rashly something as holy, and afterward to reconsider his vows" (20:25). Perhaps God would rather we say no, than to rashly say yes, then attempt to repossess our vow.

There are an abundance of places where God says for us to test the spirits, to use knowledge in our decision making, to listen to wise counsel, and to avoid being led astray. It is sound wisdom to weigh any decision we make for God, to affirm it is from the heart and that we can and will fulfill it.

In Our Homes
Retreat from Deceit
In our homes we sometimes use deceit to get what we want from our spouse, our siblings, our children, our parents, or our grandparents. We learn early on in life ways to manipulate the people we love to get what we desire. And this is an "abomination to the Lord" (20:10) just as much as the use of dishonest scales and measures to take advantage of others.

When we use deceit, or the forceful art of guilt, with members of our family, we demean their individual value. We claim that what we want tops what they want. And we degrade them with our lack of respectful treatment. A much better way is to let our desires be known in a forthright, yet humble manner. Make a request of your wife rather than a demand—tell her you wish she would cook your favorite dish, because she is so good at it, not through means of game-playing or exploitation. Ask your children to do something because it is the right thing to do, not by means of trickery. Say no at times, rather than saying yes, then not living up to your part. I believe that deceit and respect are polar opposites, if you are using deceit to get what you want within a relationship, you are unable to show respect. And if you show respect in a relationship, you will not use deceit. I have said it before, but it is worth repeating: anyone you truly love should feel important and respected in your presence.

If I were to give only one piece of advice to a couple getting married, it would be to never start using the manipulative controlling power of game-playing, but to respectfully let your hopes, dreams, desires, and needs be know through honest, upright, straightforward (yet humble) sharing of your yearnings, aspirations, and needs. The best cure for deceit is open, honest, constant communication as a way of sharing yourself with another.

I think I would be amiss if I didn't close this chapter with a statement about Proverbs 20:29. "The glory of young men is their strength, and the splendor of old men is their gray head." As an "older" man of fifty-four, I am proud of my grey hair, and I have been blessed with a lot of it. The more my hair turns gray the more I learn about relationships. While this is not true for all men, I think this saying relates to the aging process as a maturing process. As we mature, we gray, and as we grey through maturity, we begin to see life with a different vision. A vision that makes people more important than things, a vision that sees honesty as the mirror of a man, a vision that sees knowledge and wisdom as far greater than wealth, a vision that sees patience as a virtue, and a vision that waits upon the Lord and His calling before jumping into action. As a man or woman of God, ask Him to guide your every move in the home. Call upon God to make you the best father, mother, child, sibling, or friend that you can be. Then take the time to listen for His reply and act accordingly.

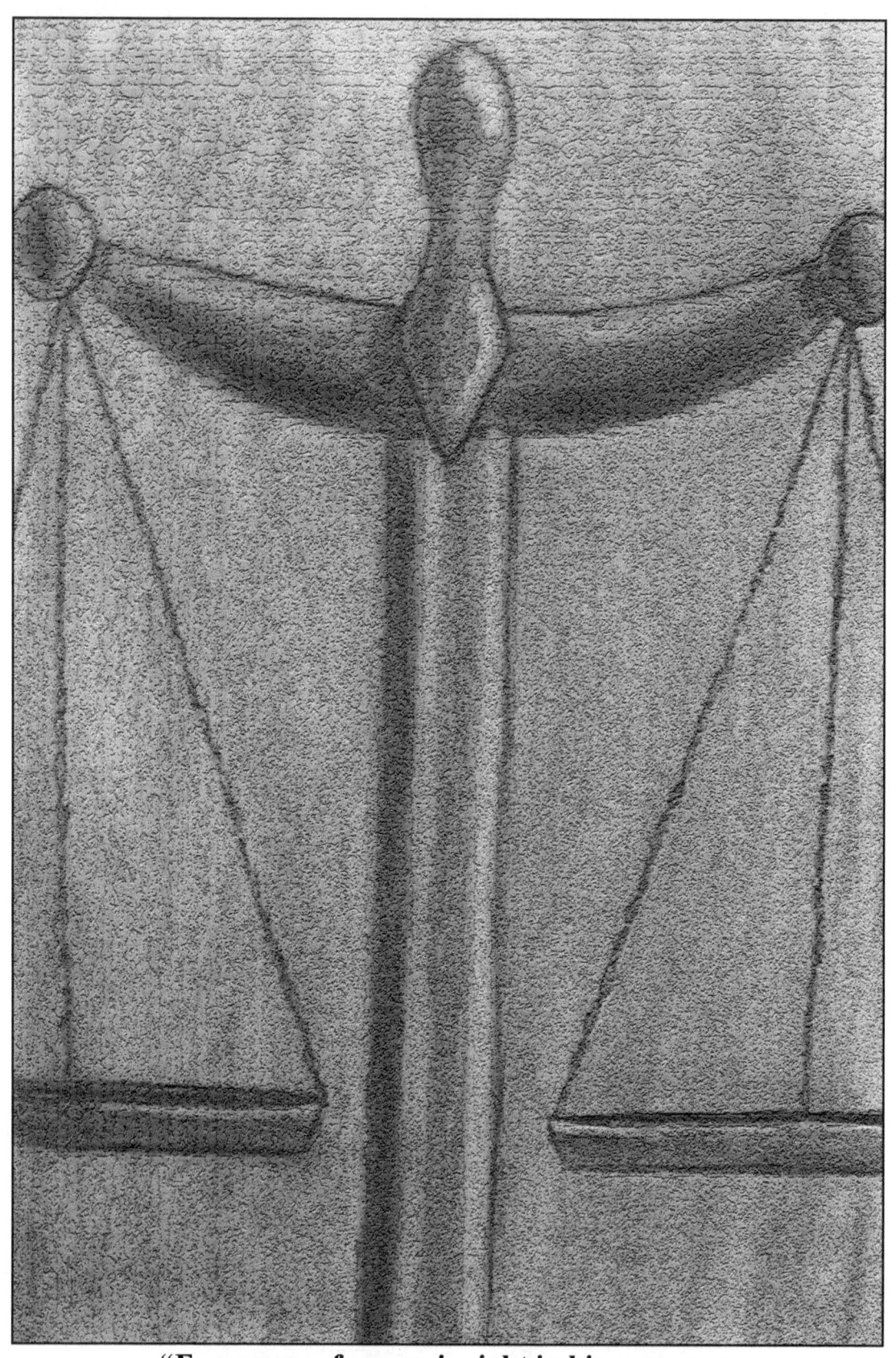

"Every way of a man is right in his own eyes,
But the LORD weighs the hearts" (21:2).

hapter 21

Proverbs 21

1 The king's heart is in
   the hand of the LORD,
   Like the rivers of water;
   He turns it wherever He wishes.
2 Every way of a man is
   right in his own eyes,
   But the LORD weighs the hearts.
3 To do righteousness and justice
   Is more acceptable to the
   LORD than sacrifice.
4 A haughty look, a proud heart,
   And the plowing of the wicked are sin.
5 The plans of the diligent lead surely to plenty,
   But those of everyone who is hasty,
   surely to poverty.
6 Getting treasures by
   a lying tongue
   Is the fleeting fantasy
   of those who seek death.
7 The violence of the
   wicked will destroy them,
   Because they refuse to do justice.
8 The way of a guilty man is perverse;
   But as for the pure, his work is right.
9 Better to dwell in a
   corner of a housetop,
   Than in a house shared
   with a contentious woman.
10 The soul of the wicked desires evil;
   His neighbor finds no favor in his eyes.
11 When the scoffer is punished,
   the simple is made wise;
   But when the wise is instructed,
   he receives knowledge.
12 The righteous God wisely
   considers the house of the wicked,
   Overthrowing the wicked for their wickedness.
13 Whoever shuts his ears to the cry of the poor
   Will also cry himself and not be heard.
14 A gift in secret pacifies anger,

And a bribe behind the back, strong wrath.

¹⁵ It is a joy for the just to do justice,
But destruction will come to the
workers of iniquity.

¹⁶ A man who wanders
from the way of understanding
Will rest in the assembly of the dead.

¹⁷ He who loves pleasure will be a poor man;
He who loves wine and oil will not be rich.

¹⁸ The wicked shall be a ransom for the righteous,
And the unfaithful for the upright.

¹⁹ Better to dwell in the wilderness,
Than with a contentious
and angry woman.

²⁰ There is desirable treasure,
And oil in the dwelling of the wise,
But a foolish man squanders it.

²¹ He who follows righteousness and mercy
Finds life, righteousness, and honor.

²² A wise man scales the city of the mighty,
And brings down the trusted stronghold.

²³ Whoever guards his mouth and tongue
Keeps his soul from troubles.

²⁴ A proud and haughty man—
"Scoffer" is his name;
He acts with arrogant pride.

²⁵ The desire of the lazy man kills him,
For his hands refuse to labor.

²⁶ He covets greedily all day long,
But the righteous gives and does not spare.

²⁷ The sacrifice of the wicked is an abomination;
How much more when he brings
it with wicked intent!

²⁸ A false witness shall perish,
But the man who hears him
will speak endlessly.

²⁹ A wicked man hardens his face,
But as for the upright, he
establishes his way.

³⁰ There is no wisdom
or understanding
Or counsel against the LORD.

³¹ The horse is prepared
for the day of battle,
But deliverance is of the LORD.

᛭   ᛭   ᛭

In the Chapter

Proverbs seems at times like a random scattering of wisdom. Chapter 21 is no different, yet there are a few sections that stand out to me.

Loving and Judging

I think most of us have heard the assertion, rather popular today, that a person should do what he thinks is best, that he is the best judge of what is right, and that we cannot say to anyone else what is or isn't the correct way to live. Proverbs 21:2 shares an interesting insight into that philosophy. This verse states that "the LORD weighs the hearts," which says two things to me: first that we must remember when making decisions that God knows what we are thinking and feeling, and second we must remember when we see the actions of others we may not always know their true intentions or motives. While we cannot sit idly by and let those we love fall to sin (as Solomon himself wrote this entire book on wisdom to discourage people from making that mistake), we also cannot see into, and therefore judge harshly, the hearts of others. Such judgment can lead to pride, something Proverbs 21:4 states clearly is sin. And, whenever we relate to others about anything, we have to guard our words carefully (21:23).

What Justice, Mercy, and Diligence Bring

This chapter speaks a lot on the idea of justice, which, paired with righteousness, is something God loves better even than a sacrifice (21:3). And yet, God also instructs us to pair righteousness with mercy (21:21). Can these two ideals sometimes seem in conflict with one another? Perhaps, but we serve a Lord who, despite the fact that we justly deserve to be stuck forever in our sinful ways, will bring us deliverance (21:31). He somehow creates a balance of justice and mercy, and if we live in wisdom, we will find this balance as well.

Verses five and twenty-five through twenty-six encourage a diligent and giving heart over laziness and greed; these latter characteristics will bring no profit to us, even though they seem to bring comfort for a time.

Beware the Angry Woman!
And then verses nine and nineteen seem to smack of a bit of humor (though complete truth) in the middle of this serious chapter. It would be better, they say, to live in a horrible or uncomfortable environment than with an argumentative, touchy, angry woman. Perhaps some women scoff at this remark: *How unfair!* they might protest. But is it not true? "A happy wife makes a happy life." "If Mama isn't happy, then nobody is happy." Many an adage that echoes these verses has become a popular saying today. For better or for worse, the attitude of a woman—and women are generally, in good ways and in bad ways, more emotionally-charged individuals—greatly affects those around her. Proverbs is not singling out women in a sexist manner, but to remind women of the great power we have over the general peace in our homes. And when we have power, we must act responsibly.

God wishes that we love and help others without a judgmental heart, that we bring justice and mercy together in our dealings with others, that we work hard and give well, and that we seek peace over argue-ability.

In Our Homes

How do those qualities speak specifically to our home lives, to our dealings with our family members?

Listen and Learn
First of all, I think we must have an open, full conversation with a family member we think may be considering an incorrect path. My husband Jay is currently looking at a job change. I was raised hearing the importance of working at a job you love (or having a happy heart if you must work, for a time, at something you do not care for in order to get to a place in your career that is fulfilling). Because I know Jay often feels more drained than uplifted by his job, I have been pressing him to take a position that seems to me, in all ways, a much better situation for him and for our family. Any time we spoke on the topic, I found foolish all his arguments to stay at his current job. I judged his motives and thought he was just being lazy and unmotivated.

Finally I asked better questions and truly listened to his concerns about the new employment. Guess what? The concerns are valid. Instead of making assumptions based on what we think has to be the best decision—because we obviously know best, right?—we need to be ready to really ask for and really hear someone else's feelings and reasons.

Setting the Example
As a still-newish parent, I am starting to learn the gravity of my actions being examples. Mercy: my mother used to explain to me that it was "not getting what we deserve." Mercy is never more important than in the home. It's too easy to give our calm and discerning selves to the world and to bring home the hammer of justice. (After all, don't we want all those strangers to think we are the nicest person ever?) But if we are an example of mercy in our homes, perhaps, when we fail, we'll be shown mercy by our family when we need it most.

Another example I must set for my sons is the importance of hard work and a giving spirit. In a society of sitting, I need to show them that rest is a reward of a diligent day's efforts. In a culture of greed, I need to show them the value of sharing and sacrifice: the best toy, the red gummy bear, the unbroken crayon (the first fruits for children).

The Peace of Pleasantness
And, finally, because I am a woman—and because I am a person—I must always try to create a feeling of peace and safety in my home. I don't want my sons or husband thinking they'd rather live on the roof or in the woods than with me!

hapter 22

Proverbs 22

¹ A good name is to be chosen
rather than great riches,
Loving favor rather
than silver and gold.
² The rich and the poor
have this in common,
The LORD is the
maker of them all.
³ A prudent man foresees
evil and hides himself,
But the simple pass on
and are punished.
⁴ By humility and the
fear of the LORD
Are riches and honor and life.
⁵ Thorns and snares are in the
way of the perverse;
He who guards his soul
will be far from them.
⁶ Train up a child in the
way he should go,
And when he is old he
will not depart from it.
⁷ The rich rules over the poor,
And the borrower is
servant to the lender.
⁸ He who sows iniquity
will reap sorrow,
And the rod of his
anger will fail.
⁹ He who has a generous
eye will be blessed,
For he gives of his
bread to the poor.
¹⁰ Cast out the scoffer, and
contention will leave;
Yes, strife and reproach will cease.
¹¹ He who loves purity of heart
And has grace on his lips,
The king will be his friend.

¹² The eyes of the LORD preserve knowledge,
   But He overthrows the words of the faithless.
¹³ The lazy man says, "There is a lion outside!
   I shall be slain in the streets!"
¹⁴ The mouth of an immoral
   woman is a deep pit;
   He who is abhorred by the
   LORD will fall there.
¹⁵ Foolishness is bound up
   in the heart of a child;
   The rod of correction
   will drive it far from him.
¹⁶ He who oppresses the
   poor to increase his riches,
   And he who gives to the rich,
   will surely come to poverty.

Sayings of the Wise
¹⁷ Incline your ear and hear
   the words of the wise,
   And apply your heart
   to my knowledge;
¹⁸ For it is a pleasant thing if
   you keep them within you;
   Let them all be fixed upon your lips,
¹⁹ So that your trust may be in the LORD;
   I have instructed you today, even you.
²⁰ Have I not written to you excellent things
   Of counsels and knowledge,
²¹ That I may make you know the
   certainty of the words of truth,
   That you may answer words of truth
   To those who send to you?
²² Do not rob the poor because he is poor,
   Nor oppress the afflicted at the gate;
²³ For the LORD will plead their cause,
   And plunder the soul of those
   who plunder them.
²⁴ Make no friendship
   with an angry man,
   And with a furious
   man do not go,
²⁵ Lest you learn his ways
   And set a snare for your soul.
²⁶ Do not be one of those who
   shakes hands in a pledge,
   One of those who is surety for debts;
²⁷ If you have nothing with which to pay,
   Why should he take away your bed

from under you?
²⁸ Do not remove the ancient landmark
Which your fathers have set.
²⁹ Do you see a man who excels in his work?
He will stand before kings;
He will not stand before unknown men.

In the Chapter
It is next to impossible to pick out only a few points in each chapter to focus on because of the wealth of wisdom in every line. However, three main points captured my attention in chapter twenty-two.

What's in a Name?
Shakespeare's Juliet contemplates this question and reasons that a person is more than his or her name. This is true, but a clean, honest, honorable name is a huge blessing. Verse one explains it is a better thing to have than money. Having a good name doesn't happen by chance, though, and it can be upheld when we make it a point in our lives to "hear the words of the wise and apply" our hearts to the knowledge shared in Proverbs (22:17).

Teach the Little Children
The Proverbs are full of instruction for parents; kids will automatically do some ridiculous or foolish things (22:15), and it is the job of a parent to "train up a child in the way he should go" (22:6), to show our children right and wrong and equip them to make appropriate choices in life.

Bothered Borrower
Again it is easy for me, an avid reader and literature professor, to reference Shakespeare, who was obviously aware of the Proverbs, as he echoes verses seven and twenty-six through twenty-seven in Polonius' advice to his son in *Hamlet*: "Neither a borrower nor a lender be." These verses explain the risks of debt: you become a servant to the one you are indebted to (22:7). And then Solomon counsels us not to purchase things we aren't able to pay for in the first place. When we do, those things don't really belong to us, and the

actual owner could come and take them away (22:26–27).

In Our Homes
Whom Do You Represent?
The connection of these pieces of advice to our households is strong. I think first of my mom's reminder in my youth as I would walk out the door to "remember who you are and whom you belong to." If we come from a family with a strong, faithful name, we must remember that we are a representation of that name in all we do, in how we live, as long as we live. As parents, we need to impress on our children the value of being a part of our family, of carrying that name. We should have pride in the wisdom of the generations that have made and kept that name respectable, and that pride should shine through and reflect upon the faces and actions of our children.

If we come from a family with a less respectable background, with things we may be ashamed of lingering in the family name, it is time to make a change, to begin to bring honor to a name that maybe didn't deserve it before.

As a wife, it can be difficult embracing your new family name. I'm always going to consider myself, for the most part, a Hilliard—because that was my upbringing, and that is where my traits and characteristics come from. But now that I have a son, and another on the way, I realize I am raising little Sextons, and how they act and react throughout life is a reflection on that family name. Jay and I want his name to grow in strength, and our example and our manner of training these boys (and any future children we may have) will affect all future generations of Sextons in our line.

My children are a representation of my family as well. Jack was named for my paternal grandfather (co-writer of this book), who said he hopes my son has a life as full as he has had. I hope my Jack can live for Jesus just as his namesake has; it's a big name to carry. And even if Jack doesn't have my dad's last name, he has his eyes, and I pray Jack can see the world in beauty and be a blessing to those around him the same as his grandfather.

And because of my respect and love of my father, I will give his name to my second son, Jonas Hilliard Sexton, who will carry the family names of both his father and mother into the future.

Training Wills
If that sounds like a huge responsibility to raise our children in a manner that brings honor to their father, father's father, and the Father, it's because, well, it is. Sometimes I look at my son and feel the weight of his future resting on my every reaction. Thankfully pieces of what I do or do not do appropriately in his upbringing will be forgotten. (I pray that the good things stick while the bad things wash out of his memory.)

I'm a worrier. I worry about being worried. I worry about making others worried. I'm sure I'll get to touch on this issue of trust in a later chapter, but at this point I want to bring up something important for worrying parents to understand: we cannot hold onto our children forever. While they are under our roofs, we must do our best to train them in God's ways, and when these children are grown, we have to live in faith and prayers that they will always follow His ways. I've already started praying that my sons will be good, that being good will come easily to them, that I will one day be with them in heaven. And in my disciplining of them, I must remember that this is the ultimate goal: to direct their life paths in the direction of Glory.

Indebted
Debt is a bit of a dirty word in my house, but I realize that I live in a culture that embraces the convenience and instant gratification of borrowing. I'd like to focus here on the wisdom and satisfaction that can come from saving before spending. Perhaps one of the reasons debt is mentioned harshly by Solomon is because it can counteract other important characteristics and life skills the author says wise people have. Debt is often the temptation of the immediate or the perceived salvation for the ill-planned.

I'm not saying we've never had to borrow before. My parents have helped us out of a few scrapes. Throughout Jay's graduate degree, we didn't take out a single student loan. We lived carefully from paycheck to paycheck, but that meant little went into savings. Soon after Jay graduated, we found a house that my eight-month-pregnant brain and heart said we needed to own. My parents helped us with the down payment, and we knew we'd get a tax refund back within two months that would allow us to repay the loan. In my normal state, I had always wanted to save up a healthy down payment before purchasing our first home, but it was hard to argue with my hormonal soon-to-be-a-mom's imposing need for more space for her coming child.

Many months later, when part of my logical brain re-engaged, I would think about the rushed decision to buy, and how perhaps we could have gotten a better deal on the house in general if we had waited until we saved up our own down payment. (Also, perhaps we would have been stuck for several months in a cramped apartment with a nursery that smelled like cat urine, so it's hard to consider all the what if's.)

With a second child coming, our current car is too small. This time, though, we are thinking and acting differently. Jay is working a second job for a couple of months, and we are putting away money to pay cash for a mini-van.

The lessons of patience, of working ahead instead of getting behind, of thinking about owning instead of owing: these are at the heart of the avoidance of debt.

Chapter 23

Proverbs 23

¹ When you sit down to eat with a ruler,
 Consider carefully what is before you;
² And put a knife to your throat
 If you are a man given to appetite.
³ Do not desire his delicacies,
 For they are deceptive food.
⁴ Do not overwork to be rich;
 Because of your own understanding, cease!
⁵ Will you set your eyes on that which is not?
 For riches certainly make themselves wings;
 They fly away like an eagle toward heaven.
⁶ Do not eat the bread of a miser,
 Nor desire his delicacies;
⁷ For as he thinks in his heart, so is he.
 "Eat and drink!" he says to you,
 But his heart is not with you.
⁸ The morsel you have eaten, you will vomit up,
 And waste your pleasant words.
⁹ Do not speak in the hearing of a fool,
 For he will despise the wisdom of your words.
¹⁰ Do not remove the ancient landmark,
 Nor enter the fields of the fatherless;
¹¹ For their Redeemer is mighty,
 He will plead their cause against you.
¹² Apply your heart to instruction,
 And your ears to words of knowledge.
¹³ Do not withhold correction from a child,
 For if you beat him with a rod, he will not die.
¹⁴ You shall beat him with a rod,
 And deliver his soul from hell.
¹⁵ My son, if your heart is wise,
 My heart will rejoice—indeed, I myself;
¹⁶ Yes, my inmost being will rejoice
 When your lips speak right things.
 Do not let your heart envy sinners,
 But be zealous for the fear of the
 LORD all the day;
¹⁸ For surely there is a hereafter,
 And your hope will not be cut off.
¹⁹ Hear, my son, and be wise;

And guide your heart in the way.
20 Do not mix with winebibbers,
   Or with gluttonous eaters of meat;
21 For the drunkard and the glutton will
   come to poverty,
   And drowsiness will clothe a man with rags.
22 Listen to your father who begot you,
   And do not despise your mother when
   she is old.
23 Buy the truth, and do not sell it,
   Also wisdom and instruction and
   understanding.
24 The father of the righteous will greatly rejoice,
   And he who begets a wise child will delight
   in him.
25 Let your father and your mother be glad,
   And let her who bore you rejoice.
26 My son, give me your heart,
   And let your eyes observe my ways.
27 For a harlot is a deep pit,
   And a seductress is a narrow well.
28 She also lies in wait as for a victim,
   And increases the unfaithful among men.
29 Who has woe?
   Who has sorrow?
   Who has contentions?
   Who has complaints?
   Who has wounds without cause?
   Who has redness of eyes?
30 Those who linger long at the wine,
   Those who go in search of mixed wine.
31 Do not look on the wine when it is red,
   When it sparkles in the cup,
   When it swirls around smoothly;
32 At the last it bites like a serpent,
   And stings like a viper.
33 Your eyes will see strange things,
   And your heart will utter perverse things.
34 Yes, you will be like one who lies down
   in the midst of the sea,
   Or like one who lies at the top of the
   mast, saying:
   "They have struck me, but I was not hurt;
   They have beaten me, but I did not feel it.
   When shall I awake, that I may seek another
   drink?"

In the Chapter
Riches on the Table and in the Pocket
Proverbs 23 begins by talking about food, and food and drink are mentioned throughout the chapter. Solomon isn't just talking about mealtime, though; he is pointing out that how one relates to these topics reflects his character. "Delicacies" can be "deceptive," and a desire for nice things can cause us to overwork ourselves, pressing ourselves to the limit for things that aren't substantial and can easily fly away like a bird (23:3–5).

Likewise, Solomon warns against spending time with or becoming a drunkard or a glutton. These people are ruled by their desires and will come to nothing (23:20–21).

Parent and Child Responsibilities
A parent cannot ignore his duties to discipline and correct his children; without early discipline, children will begin and then continue a path of poor decisions that will lead them to hell (23:13–14). On the other end, a child must listen to his parents and give them honor even unto their old age (23:22). The greatest way to bring joy to our parents is to be righteous throughout our lives, a gift appropriate to those who raised us (23:24–25).

Whom to Listen to
It can be tempting in life to listen to those who seem to be having a lot of fun, those who seduce us with what will make us happy for a short time. But these people will trap us in their sin, causing us to be unfaithful (23:27–28). Everyone has troubles, but those who try to ignore their troubles with sin will not be able to see the truth. These sins of temporary relief are alluring, but ultimately bring a destructive outcome (23:29–34).

In Our Homes
Food for Thought
Hilliards are food people. We can be at the end of a huge meal and begin talking about the next. We also often show our love for each other through food. When we dropped off my brother at college for the first time, my dad's chief vocal concern was when my brother would go get his meal

ticket. Dad needed to know his son would be well fed. And then I think about how many picture texts I send Jay of Jack eating, with little updates about his meals, and how one of my questions after I've been at work and Jay's been at home is, "What did Jack eat for lunch?"

We don't really need a fancy meal; we just need a meal to be prepared and shared in love.

Perhaps it is because I am a lover of food, born of a lover of food, that I appreciate Solomon using food as an analogy. I do think that, on one level, he is saying that a person shouldn't become obsessed with actual rich foods and drinks, but I also think he's talking about a deeper issue: if we are so concerned with the status that goes along with certain foods, we can end up focusing too much of our lives on making sure we have these foods, whatever the cost. Sharing a pot of rice and beans together as a family might be of the most value.

I cannot condemn foodies; I have a friend who is a self-proclaimed "food snob," and I judge her not. We just have to make sure we don't let the desire for anything become our master, or our hearts will be lead by status symbols, gluttony, or drunkenness instead of by the Master.

What Respect Looks Like
Too many parents today shy away from discipline, and by using the word "discipline" I am not trying to bring up a debate on spanking. Discipline is training someone in love—because of love—to follow rules, behave appropriately, and treat others with kindness. When we discipline our children, we are teaching them to have discipline in their lives, getting them to the point when they will make correct decisions on their own.

It isn't always fun, and it isn't always easy. The saying "choose your battles" has taken on a whole new meaning for me since I've had Jack. I make mistakes; I just have to pray that I am led in wisdom as I raise (which includes disciplining) my kids, and that I don't do too much damage when I don't get it right.

And for all the hard work parents put into raising their children, we children are told to have respect for our parents, even when they get older (23:22). I know not everyone has been blessed to have parents obviously deserving of respect, and I don't forget how blessed I have been. I hope that if your parents have hurt you, ignored you, or broken you, that you have someone in your life who has taken on a positive parenting role. Maybe your heart is being called to forgive your parents, or maybe you've had to break some ties, but if you have children of your own, it's time to be the parent you always needed, whether or not that is the parent you had.

When I think of what will make me the happiest in my old age, it is that my children will always want to spend time with me, and that their lives will be a beautiful devotion to their Creator as they grow and one day raise a family of their own, just as it says in Proverbs 23:25.

Be Careful Little Ears
I can remember this little song from Sunday school: "be careful little ears what you hear 'cause the Father up above is looking down in love." The people we surround ourselves with have a great impact on our decisions. Their motivations, desires, and goals will come out in how they live and what they talk about.

Jay and I have recently been incredibly blessed by joining a small group of young Christian families. We meet together weekly and often celebrate the holidays together. Being around these people, who have the same ultimate goal of living a righteous life, raising a loving family, and being a light of the Lord, is uplifting beyond what I can explain. Proverbs isn't saying we should never associate ourselves with non-Christians (Afterall, we have to go out in the world teaching people about Jesus, as proclaimed in Matthew 28:19.), but we need a solid association with those of like-minds to tell us what we need to hear (both encouragement and instruction) and give us strength to fight the daily and bigger battles of our lives as we journey with Jesus.

 hapter 24

Proverbs 24

1 Do not be envious of evil men,
   Nor desire to be with them;
2 For their heart devises violence,
   And their lips talk of troublemaking.
3 Through wisdom a house is built,
   And by understanding it is established;
4 By knowledge the rooms are filled
   With all precious and pleasant riches.
5 A wise man is strong,
   Yes, a man of knowledge
   increases strength;
6 For by wise counsel you
   will wage your own war,
   And in a multitude of
   counselors there is safety.
7 Wisdom is too lofty for a fool;
   He does not open his
   mouth in the gate.
8 He who plots to do evil
   Will be called a schemer.
9 The devising of foolishness is sin,
   And the scoffer is an abomination to men.
10 If you faint in the day of adversity,
   Your strength is small.
11 Deliver those who are
   drawn toward death,
   And hold back those
   stumbling to the slaughter.
12 If you say, "Surely we
   did not know this,"
   Does not He who weighs
   the hearts consider it?
   He who keeps your soul,
   does He not know it?
   And will He not render to
   each man according to his deeds?
13 My son, eat honey because it is good,
   And the honeycomb which is sweet
   to your taste;
14 So shall the knowledge of wisdom be

to your soul;
If you have found it, there is a prospect,
And your hope will not be cut off.
¹⁵ Do not lie in wait, O wicked man,
against the dwelling of the righteous;
Do not plunder his resting place;
¹⁶ For a righteous man
may fall seven times
And rise again,
But the wicked shall
fall by calamity.
¹⁷ Do not rejoice when your enemy falls,
And do not let your heart be glad when
he stumbles;
¹⁸ Lest the LORD see it,
and it displease Him,
And He turn away
His wrath from him.
¹⁹ Do not fret because of evildoers,
Nor be envious of the wicked;
²⁰ For there will be no prospect
for the evil man;
The lamp of the
wicked will be put out.
²¹ My son, fear the
LORD and the king;
Do not associate with
those given to change;
²² For their calamity will rise suddenly,
And who knows the ruin those two can bring?

Further Sayings of the Wise
²³ These things also belong to the wise.
It is not good to show partiality in judgment.
²⁴ He who says to the wicked, "You are righteous,"
Him the people will curse;
Nations will abhor him.
²⁵ But those who rebuke the
wicked will have delight,
And a good blessing will
come upon them.
²⁶ He who gives a right
answer kisses the lips.
²⁷ Prepare your outside work,
Make it fit for yourself in the field;
And afterward build your house.
²⁸ Do not be a witness against your
neighbor without cause,
For would you deceive with your lips?

29 Do not say, "I will do to him
just as he has done to me;
I will render to the
man according to his work."
30 I went by the field of the lazy man,
And by the vineyard of the man
devoid of understanding;
31 And there it was,
all overgrown with thorns;
Its surface was covered with nettles;
Its stone wall was broken down.
32 When I saw it, I considered it well;
I looked on it and received instruction:
33 A little sleep, a little slumber,
A little folding of the hands to rest;
34 So shall your poverty come like a prowler,
And your need like an armed man.

In the Chapter
They'll Get What's Coming to Them
Proverbs 24 begins with a warning not to envy the "evildoers" (24:1), and later repeats this advice, calling them "wicked" (24:19). These people just stir up trouble and have "no prospect" in life; they won't amount to anything (24:1, 20). One specific sin, laziness, is singled out towards the end of the chapter, and we are told that this characteristic will bring ruin. If we don't put any effort into our fields and vineyards (which are good symbols of any areas in our lives), they will become "overgrown with thorns…covered with nettles" and without protection (24:30–31). Laziness ruins purpose.

Wise Building
When we build up our homes, our families, we must do so on a foundation of true wisdom (24:3). This wisdom, Solomon has said earlier in the Proverbs, can come only from a respect for the Lord. And though some would say the riches we should fill our houses with are nice furniture and the latest technology, Proverbs says that knowledge will bring a home genuine riches (24:4), and any member of that household who seeks wisdom will also find strength (24:5).

Ignorance Isn't Bliss
Proverbs 24:10 says that if we fall when we meet adversity, it is because our strength is small. Now, verse five just said that strength comes from wisdom, so the best way to prepare ourselves for trying times is to grow in knowledge and understanding.

Perhaps one of the most difficult experiences in life is leading others to, and keeping ourselves in, Christ. I wonder if that is why delivering the sinful is mentioned right after Proverbs 24:10. And, right after that, we are told that simply saying, "I didn't know this" isn't a good enough excuse. What is "this" referring to?

Proverbs often has one piece of advice after another, not always linking verse after verse, but I can see a connection in "this" and our efforts to help others along in life. We are told time and time again in the Bible to minister to others, and Proverbs 24:12 might be saying that we cannot plead ignorance on this matter of ministry. Whatever "this" is referring to, we must be aware that God knows our hearts, and He will judge our deeds (24:12).

In Our Homes
Lazy Losers
"Well if your friends jumped off of a bridge, would you?"

It's a classic parental query with depth we ignore because we've heard it so much. Following the crowd, wanting to be like the others, keeping up with the Joneses: these are motivations for some of our unwise decisions in life. I've mentioned before, because Solomon has mentioned before, how tempting it can be to desire the lives of others, but we cannot be willing to sacrifice our salvation to be like someone else.

Also, poor decisions bring poor results. This chapter specifically mentions laziness. Laziness is not a reference to a family vacation at the beach in reward for a good school year or an evening with some downtime after a long day at work. Laziness is a mindset. Laziness lets important things in life go unattended and encourages uselessness.

No member of a working family can be lazy. We must all do our parts (finishing chores, encouraging each other, spending time together, setting and reaching goals, being conscious of the needs and feelings of each other) to create a loving environment that is a positive reflection of the Father. When people see our families, they should see a group of people whose love of the Lord is obvious in the treatment of their belongings and in their obvious sense of belonging.

The House that Jack Built
I'm not saying that you cannot find true wisdom without having children. (God uses different instances and trials in life to help us learn.) For me, though, I never had to think as much about something other than myself before I had Jack. I never knew just how selfish I was until I was forced to be selfless.

It took a tiny, screaming, demanding, difficult, beautiful, blessed, precious baby to help me understand that life is about more than my daily concerns.

Families need foundation. Abraham Lincoln said a house divided will fall. An old Sunday school song tells us that the foolish man who builds his house on sand will watch it go "splat." Solomon says our families will not stand together if we aren't established in wisdom of the Word and understanding of each other. However we learn it, we must learn to build our families on these things.

Family Comes First
When I wrote about what chapter twenty-four says on the topic of ignorance not being an excuse, I started thinking about just how important it is to minister to others. And yet, I've seen families devote themselves to benevolent activities while the needs of someone in that family goes ignored. Just like it is often easier to be on our best behavior around others, I wonder if it is sometimes easier to minister to friends and even strangers than to someone living under our own roof.

But, "charity begins at home," the old saying goes.

Though I don't remember any negatives involved in our time as foster parents, my mom tells me that part of their decision to stop was because I was crying myself to sleep every night (as a first grader, not an infant) because I wasn't able to spend any time with her. Mom and Dad had worked in foster homes for nearly seven years, and they felt that it was time to focus their efforts on something else. My parents knew their birth children needed special attention at this time. My mom continued to work, in a different position, with that children's home for ten more years, finding a different way to use her talents to serve kids in need.

As a child I was (okay, even today I am), a bit of a self-admitted attention-addict. But, I think that the extra time my parents devoted to me throughout my school years helped me stay out of trouble. I'm not saying a family is an exclusive club that ignores the needs of others; I'm not saying we should hole up in our homes and never get out to serve; I am saying that we need to keep our eyes and hearts open to the needs of our families first, and then figure out ways to serve others—together and as individuals—using our gifts to exalt the Gifter.

Chapter 25

Proverbs 25
Further Wise Sayings of Solomon
These also are proverbs of Solomon which
the men of Hezekiah king of Judah copied:
² It is the glory of God to conceal a matter,
But the glory of kings is to
search out a matter.
³ As the heavens for height
and the earthfor depth,
So the heart of kings is unsearchable.
⁴ Take away the dross from silver,
And it will go to the silversmith for jewelry.
⁵ Take away the wicked from before the king,
And his throne will be established
in righteousness.
⁶ Do not exalt yourself in
the presence of the king,
And do not stand in the
place of the great;
⁷ For it is better that
he say to you, "Come up here,"
Than that you should be put
lower in the presence of the prince,
Whom your eyes have seen.
⁸ Do not go hastily to court;
For what will you do in the end,
When your neighbor has put you to shame?
⁹ Debate your case with your neighbor,
And do not disclose the secret to another;
¹⁰ Lest he who hears it expose your shame,
And your reputation be ruined.
¹¹ A word fitly spoken
is like apples of gold
In settings of silver.
¹² Like an earring of gold
and an ornament of fine gold
Is a wise rebuker to an obedient ear.
¹³ Like the cold of snow in time of harvest
Is a faithful messenger to those who send him,
For he refreshes the soul of his masters.
¹⁴ Whoever falsely boasts of giving

Is like clouds and wind without rain.
¹⁵ By long forbearance a ruler is persuaded,
And a gentle tongue breaks a bone.
¹⁶ Have you found honey?
Eat only as much as you need,
Lest you be filled with it and vomit.
¹⁷ Seldom set foot in your neighbor's house,
Lest he become weary of you and hate you.
¹⁸ A man who bears false witness
against his neighbor
Is like a club, a sword,
and a sharp arrow.
¹⁹ Confidence in an unfaithful
man in time of trouble
Is like a bad tooth and
a foot out of joint.
²⁰ Like one who takes away
a garment in cold weather,
And like vinegar on soda,
Is one who sings songs to a heavy heart.
²¹ If your enemy is hungry, give him bread to eat;
And if he is thirsty, give him water to drink;
²² For so you will heap coals of fire on his head,
And the LORD will reward you.
²³ The north wind brings forth rain,
And a backbiting tongue an
angry countenance.
²⁴ It is better to dwell in a
corner of a housetop,
Than in a house shared
with a contentious woman.
²⁵ As cold water to a weary soul,
So is good news from a far country.
²⁶ A righteous man who falters
before the wicked
Is like a murky spring
and a polluted well.
²⁷ It is not good to eat much honey;
So to seek one's own glory is not glory.
²⁸ Whoever has no rule over his own spirit
Is like a city broken down, without walls.

In the Chapter
Haste is Waste

Proverbs 25:8–12 warns us of the dangers of hasty reactions. If someone wrongs us, our immediate response is often to seek justice, either by bringing the wrong before someone in charge who can deliver some punishment or by gossiping to others in hope of sympathy and justification for our feelings. These responses could bring us "shame" and ruin our reputations (25:8, 10). We could be considered tattlers or untrustworthy. Instead, we are told to go directly to the person who has caused the problem and try to work things out with only the offending parties.

The Proverbs here aren't telling us to ignore the problem, but to use wisdom in correcting it. We must watch our words, because careful communication is as valuable as jewelry (25:11–12).

Too Much of a Good Thing is Still Too Much
Honey is used often in the Old Testament as a symbol of reward and indulgence. Proverbs 25:16 and 27 use honey to explain the idea that we can have too much of a good thing. Honey itself is not the problem; excess is the problem. Too much honey will make a person sick (25:16).

Glory is another good thing, in it's right rite. Glory should come to us in the correct manner, and living a life with the sole purpose of seeking personal glory is meaningless because the honor we will seemingly gain is empty (25:27).

Unruly
Though verse twenty-eight is short, I was struck by it. The heart and height of true wisdom is in our abilities to discern; the result of righteous discernment should be the ability to make wise choices. When we don't have self-control, when our spirit becomes unruly, we are like a destroyed town that has no protection against future attacks.

In Our Homes
Swift to Speak: Slow to Grow
"Nobody likes a tattletale," I've heard said. Where did this statement come from? I think most of us know the feeling of insecurity that accompanies being around someone who is quick to share our every action with an authority figure. That insecurity encourages few friendships.

Being a gossip is no better a solution to solving our relationship problems. If you complain to me about a co-worker, I wonder what you say about me to others.

Tattling and gossiping are impediments to trust. These traits make the speaker seem insecure and unreliable.

Of course there are certain situations when the wrong done must be brought before someone in charge. Also, venting has its value. I can think of times I've brought up a problem to a trustworthy friend or my husband, and just the complaining out loud soothed my spirit.

The key word, of course, is a *trustworthy* friend, and the singular nature of *friend*. Once my husband Jay found out I was texting a good friend about something he had done that made me furious. His reaction wasn't what I thought it would be. He was glad. He told me he was pleased I could complain to someone who cared about me instead of sulking or bringing him every issue in our marriage. Venting to that friend often helps me find clarity in my feelings; is it something that made me angry in the moment, something that passes after talking about it, or is it something that I can process better through a conversation with a fellow Christian wife in order to bring it carefully to Jay, and not in the heat of the moment? I can answer these questions better when I vent.

We must find one or two people in our lives who will hold onto our secrets, pray with us through our frustrations, and give us the sympathetic ear we will need. We must not spread rumors or slander someone to any person who will listen (or doesn't want to listen but is stuck waiting to use the copier after us). If we need to complain about our spouses, we should make sure it is to someone who understands that we are committed to our marriage.

No relationship, with family, friends, or co-workers, is going to be problem-free. Solomon tells us to use wisdom in how we approach these troubles, and we will find reward.

Sweetness Overload

Since I'm not the biggest fan of honey, I mentally substitute one of my favorite sweets into Proverbs 25:16 and 27—peach cobbler, perhaps, or banana pudding. When I was young, my grandparents were always impressed with how much food I could put away for a little girl. "We keep feeding her, and she keeps asking for more!" they exclaimed one day. And on that day I gorged myself until I was literally sick. At first, I'm sure the enjoyment of eating everything I wanted without my mom's protest seemed like the best freedom I had ever experienced. But I learned a quick lesson: there is a reason behind the rule of quantity my mom established.

A wise person sees that free will is not doing what you want: it is the freedom to decide to do what is best.

A household without rules will not function, but a house with too many rules will seem like a prison. As parents, we have to find the balance, so that the sweet things in life are recognized as blessings and are never abused or overused. As children, we have to think a little differently about the rules in our household. Most of the time rules aren't set as a punishment or with the intent to keep us from fun; wise rules are in place to prevent chaos, provide safety, and promote success—for every member and the family as a whole.

The Best Defense

Protection: one of my main objectives as a parent. Right now, Jack has few walls of defense—he can scream, and he is learning to vocalize his problems, requests, and pains. I can watch as his young brain tries to process cause and effect. (Even while writing those few sentences, I had to pause to rescue him from a precarious situation as he had been climbing in the underside of a little stool, bent over too far, and became stuck. I answered his call of "Hold you, me," which means "Hold me, please," and saved him from his small crisis.) Jack is about twenty-two months old. He needs me to help him see right from wrong, and to untangle him from his mistakes.

One day, though, we all must learn how to rule our own spirits. I don't think this learning process ends the day we move away from home. I don't think there is a particular rite of passage (such as our baptism or graduation or wedding—which are all important ceremonies honoring and acknowledging a commitment fulfilled) that suddenly means we have spirit-self-control. A lifelong battle is before us, a battle of taking the right path in life.

We can establish certain lines of defense to help us along the way, though, and the entire book of Proverbs is like a guidebook for setting up these lines. Temptations are everywhere. The best defense is to be ready for the offense.

hapter 26

Proverbs 26

1 As snow in summer and rain in harvest,
   So honor is not fitting for a fool.
2 Like a flitting sparrow, like a flying swallow,
   So a curse without cause shall not alight.
3 A whip for the horse,
   A bridle for the donkey,
   And a rod for the fool's back.
4 Do not answer a fool
   according to his folly,
   Lest you also be like him.
5 Answer a fool according to his folly,
   Lest he be wise in his own eyes.
6 He who sends a message by the hand of a fool
   Cuts off his own feet and drinks violence.
7 Like the legs of the lame that hang limp
   Is a proverb in the mouth of fools.
8 Like one who binds a stone in a sling
   Is he who gives honor to a fool.
9 Like a thorn that goes into
   the hand of a drunkard
   Is a proverb in the mouth of fools.
10 The great God who formed everything
   Gives the fool his hire and the
   transgressor his wages.
11 As a dog returns to his own vomit,
   So a fool repeats his folly.
12 Do you see a man wise in his own eyes?
   There is more hope for a fool than for him.
13 The lazy man says, "There is a
   lion in the road!
   A fierce lion is in the streets!"
14 As a door turns on its hinges,
   So does the lazy man on his bed.
15 The lazy man buries his hand in the bowl;
   It wearies him to bring it back to his mouth.
16 The lazy man is wiser in his own eyes
   Than seven men who can answer sensibly.
17 He who passes by and meddles
   in a quarrel not his own
   Is like one who takes a dog by the ears.

¹⁸ Like a madman who throws
   firebrands, ar-rows, and death,
¹⁹ Is the man who deceives his neighbor,
   And says, "I was only joking!"
²⁰ Where there is no wood,
   the fire goes out;
   And where there is no
   talebearer, strife ceases.
²¹ As charcoal is to burning
   coals, and wood to fire,
   So is a contentious man to kindle strife.
²² The words of a talebearer are like tasty trifles,
   And they go down into the inmost body.
²³ Fervent lips with a wicked heart
   Are like earthenware
   covered with silver dross.
²⁴ He who hates, disguises it with his lips,
   And lays up deceit within himself;
²⁵ When he speaks kindly, do not believe him,
   For there are seven abominations in his heart;
²⁶ Though his hatred is covered by deceit,
   His wickedness will be revealed
   before the assembly.
²⁷ Whoever digs a pit will fall into it,
   And he who rolls a stone will have
   it roll back on him.
²⁸ A lying tongue hates
   those who are crushed by it,
   And a flattering mouth works ruin.

In the Chapter
What Wisdom is NOT
Proverbs chapter twenty-six is pretty well divided into four categories of mankind: the fool, the sloth, the meddler, and the loather—each of these will never find wisdom because he is too caught up in his sin.

The Fool
The fool deserves no honor, and he is a slave to his stupidity (26:1, 8, 3). He cannot be trusted and should not be treated as having wisdom (26: 6, 5). If he does attempt to share wisdom, it is useless and can even bring harm (26:7, 9). And yet, Solomon says that "there is more hope for a fool" than for a man who overestimates his wisdom (26:12).

Even though the fool will continually make poor decisions (26:11), he is deemed as having more of a chance than someone who considers himself quite wise. Solomon calls us to wisdom, and here he warns us against an inflated self-view. There is always more for the wise to learn.

The Sloth
The Proverbs speak often against the evils of laziness. A lazy man will call out danger, but he won't do anything about it (26:13). What can we expect from someone who is so avidly against hard work that he finds feeding himself a chore (26:15)? And again the Proverbs warn us against calling ourselves wise; the lazy man thinks he is wise, after all, even though others give better advice and answers (26:16).

The Meddler
The meddler is one who involves himself in "quarrel[s] not his own" (26:17). He disguises his deceit as humor (26:19). He is fuel for the fire of strife in the lives of others (26:20–21). But, we might ask, how does he get so much power over the lives of those around him? His words "are like tasty trifles, and they go down into the inmost body," meaning that he knows what to say, and how to say it (26:22). The meddler understands the human spirit enough to manipulate it, making him a vicious acquaintance.

The Loather
The man with hate and wickedness in his heart may not be easy to spot because he covers it up with "fervent lips" and kind words (26:23 –25). But his "flattering mouth works ruin" because his feelings and words are not sincere (26:28). One day his true nature and his lies will be revealed, but until then we must be cautious of people whose lives are covered up with loathing (26:26).

In Our Homes
Fool's Gold
The sloth, the meddler, and the loather: all of these people have foolishness at the root of their problem. Somehow lazy people find it more prudent to waste their lives away on nothing; meddlers thrive on stirring up and continuing on the drama of others; and the loathers think that, in-

stead of working through their hurt, they should mask it in false words. None of these lives are built on wisdom, and we must avoid taking on these roles in our homes.

What is so tempting about being foolish? In part, it is an escape. The problem arises when the brief escapes from life's hardships turn into lifestyles of sin. A rest from stress becomes a habit of time wasted; helping another person with a quarrel becomes a secret enjoyment of watching others quarrel; a pain we'd rather not think about becomes a heart hard against one person and then, perhaps, all people. It only takes that first unattended step in the direction of foolishness to begin a life journey along that way.

Yes, we must rest, aid, feel, but we have to do all of these things with a heart rooted in wisdom—which is a heart rooted in God's Word. We should keep a careful prayer life that includes asking God for wisdom in our dealings with our family and our friends, and in asking God for wisdom to be given as a blessing to our children.

And remember, wisdom is not walking around thinking we are so smart: it's knowing there is always more to learn about becoming more Christlike, and working our best always at achieving that goal. No foolish, lazy, meddling, loathsome spirit would even try.

# Chapter 27

Proverbs 27

1 Do not boast about tomorrow,
  For you do not know what a
  day may bring forth.
2 Let another man praise you,
  and not your own mouth;
  A stranger, and not your own lips.
3 A stone is heavy and sand is weighty,
  But a fool's wrath is heavier than
  both of them.
4 Wrath is cruel and anger a torrent,
  But who is able to stand before jealousy?
5 Open rebuke is better
  Than love carefully concealed.
6 Faithful are the wounds of a friend,
  But the kisses of an enemy are deceitful.
7 A satisfied soul loathes the honeycomb,
  But to a hungry soul every bitter
  thing is sweet.
8 Like a bird that wanders from its nest
  Is a man who wanders from his place.
9 Ointment and perfume delight the heart,
  And the sweetness of a man's friend gives
  delight by hearty counsel.
10 Do not forsake your own
  friend or your father's friend,
  Nor go to your brother's house
  in the day of your calamity;
  Better is a neighbor nearby than
  a brother far away.
11 My son, be wise, and
  make my heart glad,
  That I may answer him
  who reproaches me.
12 A prudent man foresees
  evil and hides himself;
  The simple pass on and are punished.
13 Take the garment of him who is
  surety for a stranger,
  And hold it in pledge
  when he is surety for a seductress.

¹⁴ He who blesses his friend with a loud
   voice, rising early in the morning,
   It will be counted a curse to him.
¹⁵ A continual dripping on a very rainy day
   And a contentious woman are alike;
¹⁶ Whoever restrains her restrains the wind,
   And grasps oil with his right hand.
¹⁷ As iron sharpens iron,
   So a man sharpens the
   countenance of his friend.
¹⁸ Whoever keeps the fig
   tree will eat its fruit;
   So he who waits on his
   master will be honored.
¹⁹ As in water face reflects face,
   So a man's heart reveals the man.
²⁰ Hell and Destruction are never full;
   So the eyes of man are never satisfied.
²¹ The refining pot is for silver and
   the furnace for gold,
   And a man is valued by
   what others say of him.
²² Though you grind a fool in a mortar
   with a pestle along with crushed grain,
   Yet his foolishness will not depart from him.
²³ Be diligent to know the state of your flocks,
   And attend to your herds;
²⁴ For riches are not forever,
   Nor does a crown endure
   to all generations.
²⁵ When the hay is removed, and
   the tender grass shows itself,
   And the herbs of the
   mountains are gathered in,
²⁶ The lambs will provide your clothing,
   And the goats the price of a field;
²⁷ You shall have enough goats'
   milk for your food,
   For the food of your household,
   And the nourishment of your maidservants.

༄ ༄ ༄

In the Chapter
Let Others Say It
   "A man is valued by what others say of him" (Proverbs 27:21). This is a clear and powerful verse. Remember that Proverbs 21 told us that

only God can truly weigh the hearts of man, but Proverbs 27 contains several verses that tell us the consequence of our reputations, of what others say and think about us. Try as we might, we cannot hide; our hearts will reflect our true selves just like water reflects our faces (27:19).

Because of the importance of what others say about us, we could be tempted to loudly proclaim our good deeds—just to be sure none of our efforts go unnoticed, of course—but self-praise is worthless. Merit is found only in the praise of others, perhaps even strangers, who witness our actions and deem them worthy (27:2).

Friendship on Stormy Waters
One of the best blessings of this life is having good friends. Friends stick with each other (27:10). Proverbs 27:9 explains that a good friendship is like ointment (which heals) and perfume (which enhances or sweetens) because a friend is there to give "hearty counsel." When we are having a hard time, we might think first of seeking solace in family members, but, as we grow older, families can move away from each other. We shouldn't underestimate the help that can come from our neighbors (27:10).

Proverbs 27:17 brings to mind the image of a blacksmith, shaping and sharpening one piece of iron with another. In the same way, Solomon says, a friend affects his friend's "countenance," a word the dictionary explains can mean appearance, facial expression, composure, or support. Friends have a powerful influence: we must pick wise friends; we must be wise friends.

In Our Homes
Reputable Reputation
I wrote earlier about being conscious of how our decisions reflect upon our family names; now we have to consider how those same decisions reflect upon our own name. Keeping our reputations in check has two motives: one selfish and one selfless.

Most people care about what others think about them. This perhaps selfish concern can be harvested for good results. Though we shouldn't do good things only because we want to be viewed as good, this desire can be a starting place for positive decisions. Of course, worry about fitting in can also be the starting place for poor decisions, which brings us to a deeper motive: the knowledge that our reputations are a direct representation of our faith. Yes, we will make mistakes. We must pray that these mistakes show through as our humanity rather than weaken God's greatness in the eyes of others.

We will be judged by our hearts, our actions, our words. These judgments will lead others to talk about us. This talk will form our reputations. These reputations will affect our ministry.

Friends are Extended Family
"Sometimes we are a little overwhelmed with the idea of how blessed we are to be a part of this group. You are an answer to prayers we didn't even know we were making."

This is something I wrote today as an online posting to the small group of Christian friends I mentioned earlier. I also wrote online that I was "looking around myself and realizing that God has been building up a strong defense in our lives to make us better equipped to handle this coming baby. It still may be like being thrown into a deep pool, but at least there are multiple life rafts to swim to." I acknowledge that I mixed my metaphors in that latter quote, but both are strong images I keep seeing lately.

When we had Jack, we didn't have the most solid support system. We were surrounded by young, single friends and couples who didn't have children, and we both struggled to keep these friendships alive. Don't get me wrong; several of these friends would have done anything we could have ever asked for—but we honestly didn't know what we needed enough to ask. Friendships crumbled. We crumbled. If it wasn't for my parents and their help, I don't know what I would have done. But, as valuable as parents are, they are not the same as having friends who are in a similar situation in life.

The other image is of drowning, which I continually thought of during those first several months of motherhood. Since I had let most of my friendships fall away, I sunk deeper and deeper. Fear of a similar outcome kept me worried about ever having a second child, but my planning came to nothing: God had other plans.

I'm almost in the third trimester, awaiting the birth of our second son, and I have finally noticed that God's plans didn't mean He was giving us another child and walking away. He's been preparing our family's growth for the past year as we have developed new friendships and as some of our old friends have started having babies of their own.

I remember watching other new moms and wondering how they had the strength to spend time with their friends with all that motherhood takes out of you; I now see that the friendships are the strength.

Solid friendships are an extension of family, a blessing from God, a defense against the hardships of the world, a life raft when the waves threaten to cover us, and a source of strength and solace when we are in need.

 hapter 28

Proverbs 28

1 The wicked flee when no one pursues,
  But the righteous are bold as a lion.
2 Because of the transgression
  of a land, many are its princes;
  But by a man of understanding
  and knowledge
  Right will be prolonged.
3 A poor man who oppresses the poor
  Is like a driving rain which leaves no food.
4 Those who forsake the law praise the wicked,
  But such as keep the law contend with them.
5 Evil men do not understand justice,
  But those who seek the LORD understand all.
6 Better is the poor who walks in his integrity
  Than one perverse in his ways, though
  he be rich.
7 Whoever keeps the law
  is a discerning son,
  But a companion of gluttons
  shames his father.
8 One who increases his possessions
  by usury and extortion
  Gathers it for him who
  will pity the poor.
9 One who turns away his ear
  from hearing the law,
  Even his prayer is an abomination.
10 Whoever causes the upright to go
  astray in an evil way,
  He himself will fall into his own pit;
  But the blameless will inherit good.
11 The rich man is wise in his own eyes,
  But the poor who has understanding
  searches him out.
12 When the righteous rejoice,
  there is great glory;
  But when the wicked arise,
  men hide themselves.
13 He who covers his sins will not prosper,
  But whoever confesses and forsakes them will

have mercy.
¹⁴ Happy is the man who
is always reverent,
But he who hardens his
heart will fall into calamity.
¹⁵ Like a roaring lion and a charging bear
Is a wicked ruler over poor people.
¹⁶ A ruler who lacks understanding
is a great oppressor,
But he who hates
covetousness will prolong his days.
¹⁷ A man burdened with bloodshed
will flee into a pit;
Let no one help him.
¹⁸ Whoever walks blamelessly
will be saved,
But he who is perverse in
his ways will suddenly fall.
¹⁹ He who tills his land will have
plenty of bread,
But he who follows frivolity
will have poverty enough!
²⁰ A faithful man will abound
with blessings,
But he who hastens to be
rich will not go unpunished.
²¹ To show partiality is not good,
Because for a piece of bread a
man will transgress.
²² A man with an evil eye hastens after riches,
And does not consider that poverty will
come upon him.
²³ He who rebukes a man will
find more favor afterward
Than he who flatters with the tongue.
²⁴ Whoever robs his father or his mother,
And says, "It is no transgression,"
The same is companion to a destroyer.
²⁵ He who is of a proud heart stirs up strife,
But he who trusts in the LORD
will be prospered.
²⁶ He who trusts in his
own heart is a fool,
But whoever walks
wisely will be delivered.
²⁷ He who gives to the
poor will not lack,
But he who hides his
eyes will have many curses.

28 When the wicked arise, men hide themselves;
But when they perish, the righteous increase.

In the Chapter
Wicked vs. Righteous
Proverbs 28:1 begins by telling us that the wicked run even when no one is after them—which makes me wonder if they are burdened with a guilty conscious on some level, whether they recognize it or not. Also, they are cowards at heart, because those praised as bold are the opposite of wicked: they are "righteous" (28:1).

Another difference between these two categories of people is that when evil people are around, others hide, while the honorable man brings glory through his rejoicing spirit (28:12, 28). In the end, Proverbs explains that we cannot conceal our secrets; we have to confess in order to find mercy (28:13). And not only will we find mercy as the reward of coming clean and living a virtuous life, we also have the hope that the wicked will soon fall away, as the righteous will grow in number and strength (28:28).

Law and Order
Another topic Proverbs 28 repeatedly raises is the importance of the law, and how those with wisdom and discernment follow governing principles (28:7). Breaking rules is siding with and giving strength to the wicked, who don't understand integrity or justice (28:4–5). If we ignore regulations, our prayers will have no validity, but upholding the law will bring us understanding (28:9, 5).

Rich vs. Poor
Riches may seem like the ultimate reward, but they can become a huge distraction from living a wise life. Integrity can be harder to obtain for the affluent, because riches are often gained through perverse ways, such as extortion of others, and can take over the hearts of those hastening to become wealthy (28:6, 8, 20, 22). A rich man may think he is wise, but if he "follows frivolity," he will come to ruin (28:11, 19).

It is better to have integrity, work hard, be faithful, and give to others—even if that doesn't make us rich (28:6, 19, 20, 22, 27). Our ultimate trust has to be in our Father; faithfulness to Him is the only way to truly prosper and become richly blessed (28:25, 20).

In Our Homes
Hide and Seek
A common childhood game—hide and seek—where the one who is "it" must count to a designated number and then search out those who have hidden away: it's fun for sport, but how many of us would like it if people hid every time we came near? Honestly, I can think of a few people I wouldn't mind hiding from me, but, in general, I want to be the type of person people are glad to see—someone who brings brilliance and grandeur with me wherever I go. This includes my own home.

Proverbs explains that the only way to give off this kind of greatness is to live righteously. While the wicked hide from adversity and cause others to hide from them, the righteous rejoice and aren't afraid to admit their mistakes.

My husband has warned me against my tendency to dwell on the disagreeable. About a year after Jack was born, I started making daily goals; one of them was to be more positive. My natural tendency may be to jump on the unpleasant, so I have to fight that urge, or quickly follow my negative statements with something positive.

Of course all negatives cannot be avoided, but I want my house to be a center of positivity—a place my children find to be obviously overwhelmed with the blessings of God. And when I do make mistakes, I should seek forgiveness and change my ways, so that I can be an example of this mind-set that Proverbs names as belonging to the righteous one: the one who is bold, the one who is surrounded by glory because of her actions and attitude (28:1, 20).

Rules Aren't for Losers
Rules have a reason; they create order, balance,

and safety. I wrote in chapter twenty-five about changing our outlook on rules. Proverbs 28 brings up two important points about ignoring the law: it increases the strength of the wicked and decreases the strength of our prayers.

Consider this: if you knew someone was defying you, and that person kept coming to ask you for favors, how apt would you be to help? God has more strength in His mercy than man does, but that example opens my eyes to how a clean life can create a cleaner avenue for prayer.

As children, we shouldn't follow the rules of our parents (or of the Father) only to get something in return. Proverbs isn't encouraging manipulation or quid-pro-quo. We should obey God, and our parents, because it is a sign of respect. And, as parents, we shouldn't demand reverence because we have an established right to it: we should, instead, live in a manner that honors and deserves that respect.

Riches and Ruin
A greatly misquoted Bible verse is 1 Timothy 6:10. The popular line is "money is the root of all evil," when, in fact, the verse actually says, "The love of money is the root of *all kinds of* evil" (emphasis added). In Proverbs 28 Solomon again points out the tempting powers of riches. Just as the honey in Proverbs 25, so can the pursuit of wealth divert us from our true life goals as Christians.

As I've already touched on that topic, I want to look in a different direction, focusing on the word "frivolity" (28:19). Frivolity is not a path taken only by the rich; in fact, frivolity can be the very thing keeping a family from creating a secure financial status. People who have little, people who have a lot—anyone can waste; anyone can claim there isn't enough. I've watched families make financial blunder after blunder because they couldn't manage money. "If we made more, we'd be all right," they say. Sometimes the amount you make does dictate your financial struggles. Recently a friend of mine named Tim Smith showed the other side, though, when he told me that if you make more, or make less, you'll spend it. It makes me think that if you are unwise with little, you'd probably be unwise with a lot.

Financial security for your family is a noble goal. It shouldn't be obtained by trickery or dishonesty or miser-hood, though. And wisdom in saving and spending should be a family task. Children should be taught how to handle money and budget by parents who set the example.

We cannot be distracted in life by the desire for riches, we cannot claim to be piously poor while we are, in fact, wasting God's gifts and destroying security for our family, and we cannot even claim that a trust in the Lord to provide is the reason for our poor financial decisions. (God did provide, and we squandered it.) None of these lifestyles show a faithfulness and appreciation for God's blessings, and all of them will leave us feeling poor.

(As an afternote to this scathing entry on money, I have to admit that the words shared were just as much a reminder for me to be wiser in my spending as they were a message for the reader.)

hapter 29

Proverbs 29

[1] He who is often rebuked,
   and hardens his neck,
   Will suddenly be destroyed,
   and that without remedy.
[2] When the righteous are in
   authority, the people rejoice;
   But when a wicked man rules,
   the people groan.
[3] Whoever loves wisdom
   makes his father rejoice,
   But a companion of harlots
   wastes his wealth.
[4] The king establishes the land by justice,
   But he who receives bribes overthrows it.
[5] A man who flatters his neighbor
   Spreads a net for his feet.
[6] By transgression an evil man is snared,
   But the righteous sings and rejoices.
[7] The righteous considers the cause of the poor,
   But the wicked does not understand
   such knowledge.
[8] Scoffers set a city aflame,
   But wise men turn away wrath.
[9] If a wise man contends
   with a foolish man,
   Whether the fool rages or
   laughs, there is no peace.
[10] The bloodthirsty hate the blameless,
   But the upright seek his well-being.
[11] A fool vents all his feelings,
   But a wise man holds them back.
[12] If a ruler pays attention to lies,
   All his servants become wicked.
[13] The poor man and the oppressor
   have this in common:
   The LORD gives light to the eyes of both.
[14] The king who judges the poor with truth,
   His throne will be established forever.
[15] The rod and rebuke give wisdom,
   But a child left to himself brings shame

to his mother.
16 When the wicked are
multiplied, transgression increases;
But the righteous will see their fall.
17 Correct your son, and he will give you rest;
Yes, he will give delight to your soul.
18 Where there is no revelation,
the people cast off restraint;
But happy is he who keeps the law.
19 A servant will not be corrected
by mere words;
For though he understands,
he will not respond.
20 Do you see a man hasty in his words?
There is more hope for a fool than for him.
21 He who pampers his servant from childhood
Will have him as a son in the end.
22 An angry man stirs up strife,
And a furious man abounds
in transgression.
23 A man's pride will
bring him low,
But the humble in spirit
will retain honor.
24 Whoever is a partner with a
thief hates his own life;
He swears to tell the truth,
but reveals nothing.
25 The fear of man brings a snare,
But whoever trusts in the
LORD shall be safe.
26 Many seek the ruler's favor,
But justice for man comes
from the LORD.
27 An unjust man is an
abomination to the righteous,
And he who is upright in the way
is an abomination to the wicked.

☙   ☙   ☙

In the Chapter
Criticism
Proverbs 29:1 begins with double ideas about criticism. It says that if someone is often rebuked and becomes hardened to the scolding, he will be destroyed. As those in submission, we can read this as a reminder to keep ourselves open to con-

structive criticism: it can help us make important changes in our life that will keep us from destruction. As those in authority, we can read this to mean that we shouldn't constantly berate a person, because it can make him ignore our suggestions when they are needed most for important correction.

Handing out the appropriate amount of praise and punishment, critique and compliments, marks a good ruler. A good ruler will make the people rejoice (29:2); he knows how to treat those working under him well enough that they become like his sons (29:21). And though Proverbs 29:21 mentions "pampering," a balance in pampering and "correction" (29:17) is obviously needed.

In the end, we have to remember that the ultimate ruler is the Lord, who will bring justice and safety to those who trust in Him (29:26, 25).

Tongue-tied, on Purpose
Proverbs mentions often the importance of watching our words. In Proverbs 29, we are told that those who ridicule and make fun "set a city aflame" (29:8). The wise, instead, know that teasing and taunting can breed anger, and they work hard to "turn away wrath" (29:8). The wise also are careful with letting their feelings come out verbally, while the foolish always say exactly how they feel (29:11). We are told to think before we speak—a fool has better chances in life than someone quick to talk (29:20).

In Our Homes
Give and Take
Balance: every home needs balance. I've used the word before concerning rules, and I'll use it again concerning reproof. We cannot spend all day giving idle praise; we cannot push constant condemnation. No one wants to listen when all he hears are negatives. False positivity can lead to false hope.

Some people find it easier to give compliments, and others correction. But we have to see the value of both—as those who give and those who receive. Words affect me greatly, as is made obvious by my career path in communication, writing, and literature. I understand and feel the subtleties of words—their meaning, intent, and inflection. I feel the value of a compliment and the harshness of a reprimand. It's important to know how those in your family are affected by your words, as some will be even more sensitive than others.

One week a female friend and I decided to take on the challenge of praising our husbands without limit. For me, it wasn't easy. Sometimes when my mouth said, "Thanks for putting away the laundry," my heart said, *Though you never say thank you when I do it all the time.* But, I was a little surprised by the response I got throughout the week. I figured all that praise would make Jay think he was doing a splendid job doing little, but instead it became an encouragement to do more…without my asking! Yes, my husband who claims that he doesn't need verbal affirmation became more helpful around the house just because he felt noticed and acknowledged.

Praising our children might seem easier; every little accomplishment can honestly astound us. But we cannot ignore the times we must help them change their behavior. Correction is a must: we have to be ready to give and receive it. But correction shouldn't be the sole goal of our parenting, or our children will stop listening.

A House of Kindness and Support
Our homes are like our own little city or community, and the last thing we want to do is set our family "aflame" by ridiculing each other (29:8).

"Sticks and stones may break my bones, but words will never hurt me" is an untrue chant. Words do hurt—both those meant to sting and those meant to tease. Most humor comes from a true feeling, and teasing someone can be a sign of defensiveness, insecurity, or cruelty. We don't want any of those motives in our homes.

My brother and I weren't allowed to make fun of each other; our treatment of one another was supposed to reflect respect, and I am grateful for my parents' institution of this ideal. Teasing too often hits on a painful nerve; teasers too often know just the right words that hurt, though they hide it under the guise of a joke. Taunting can bring anger, which the Proverbs say the wise "turn away" (29:8).

Our homes should be a place of safety: a place each member goes to be uplifted and encouraged. Life is hard—our treatment of those we love shouldn't be.

"And man is driven. The ship's movement through the sea makes me think about how man's mind works to solve problems."

 hapter 30

Proverbs 30
The Wisdom of Agur
¹ The words of Agur the son
   of Jakeh, his utterance.
   This man declared to Ithiel—
   to Ithiel and Ucal:
² Surely I am more
   stupid than any man,
   And do not have the
   understanding of a man.
³ I neither learned wisdom
   Nor have knowledge
   of the Holy One.
⁴ Who has ascended into
   heaven, or descended?
   Who has gathered the
   wind in His fists?
   Who has bound the
   waters in a garment?
   Who has established all
   the ends of the earth?
   What is His name, and what
   is His Son's name,
   If you know?
⁵ Every word of God is pure;
   He is a shield to those who
   put their trust in Him.
⁶ Do not add to His words,
   Lest He rebuke you,
   and you be found a liar.
⁷ Two things I request of You
   (Deprive me not before I die):
⁸ Remove falsehood and lies far from me;
   Give me neither poverty nor riches—
   Feed me with the food allotted to me;
⁹ Lest I be full and deny You,
   And say, "Who is the LORD?"
   Or lest I be poor and steal,
   And profane the name of my God.
¹⁰ Do not malign a servant to his master,
   Lest he curse you, and you be found guilty.

¹¹ There is a generation that curses its father,
   And does not bless its mother.
¹² There is a generation that
   is pure in its own eyes,
   Yet is not washed from its filthiness.
¹³ There is a generation—oh,
   how lofty are their eyes!
   And their eyelids are lifted up.
¹⁴ There is a generation whose
   teeth are like swords,
   And whose fangs are like knives,
   To devour the poor from off the earth,
   And the needy from among men.
¹⁵ The leech has two daughters—
   Give and Give!
   There are three things
   that are never satisfied,
   Four never say, "Enough!":
¹⁶ The grave,
   The barren womb,
   The earth that is not satisfied with water—
   And the fire never says, "Enough!"
¹⁷ The eye that mocks his father,
   And scorns obedience to his mother,
   The ravens of the valley will pick it out,
   And the young eagles will eat it.
¹⁸ There are three things which
   are too wonderful for me,
   Yes, four which I do not understand:
¹⁹ The way of an eagle in the air,
   The way of a serpent on a rock,
   The way of a ship in the midst of the sea,
   And the way of a man with a virgin.
²⁰ This is the way of an adulterous woman:
   She eats and wipes her mouth,
   And says, "I have done no wickedness."
²¹ For three things the earth is perturbed,
   Yes, for four it cannot bear up:
²² For a servant when he reigns,
   A fool when he is filled with food,
²³ A hateful woman when she is married,
   And a maidservant who
   succeeds her mistress.
²⁴ There are four things
   which are little on the earth,
   But they are exceedingly wise:
²⁵ The ants are a people not strong,
   Yet they prepare their food in the summer;
²⁶ The rock badgers are a feeble folk,

Yet they make their homes in the crags;
27 The locusts have no king,
Yet they all advance in ranks;
28 The spider skillfully grasps
with its hands,
And it is in kings' palaces.
29 There are three things which
are majestic in pace,
Yes, four which are stately in walk:
30 A lion, which is mighty among beasts
And does not turn away from any;
31 A greyhound,
A male goat also,
And a king whose troops are with him.
32 If you have been foolish in exalting yourself,
Or if you have devised evil, put your hand
on your mouth.
33 For as the churning of milk produces butter,
And wringing the nose produces blood,
So the forcing of wrath produces strife.

In the Chapter
Agur Counts: Two Blessings Requested
Proverbs 30 is attributed to the writer Agur, who is introduced in the first verse as being "the son of Jakeh." Throughout the chapter, Agur follows the writing trend of counting off different items. I would like to explore a couple of these. The first counting is the two things he requests before he dies. First, he asks to be surrounded in truth, for deceit to be far from him (30:8).

Second, he asks for a moderate amount of wealth—"neither poverty nor riches" (30:8). He recognizes that riches, that being full, may make him forget the Lord (30:9). On the other hand, poverty may bring him to a desperate state where he would steal or curse God (30:9).

Agur wants to trust in the Lord, whom he lists in verse four as having great powers over the earth and whose every word is pure (30:4, 5). Agur understands that a life of extreme wealth or destitution could distract him from this trust.

Agur Counts: Satisfaction
Proverbs 30:15–16 talk about things that are "never satisfied," that always demand, "Give and Give!" An interesting note, the four things mentioned work in pairs: death and the inability to create life; the need for water and the consuming flames of a fire (30:16).

All remind me of emptiness, which is the root of longing, and ending. But we do not have to fear an empty life or our end, because, though the debt of our sin is death, God has offered us salvation through Jesus (Romans 6:23). Christ has given us an escape from the all-consuming nature of these things through His sacrifice which "abolished death and brought life and immortality to light through the Gospel" (2 Timothy 1:10).

Agur Counts: Wonderment
Then, Agur mentions things he marvels at. Two involve nature—an eagle in the air and a snake on a stone—and two the nature of man—our drive to success and progress and our sexual drive (30:18–20). As he mentions God's power over nature in verse four, and mentions here wondering at animals, I think we see that Agur is aware of God's influence in the natural world. God made the entire creation, man being only one part of that creation.

And man is driven. The ship's movement through the sea makes me think about how man's mind works to solve problems (30:19). It is a marvel what man is able to construct as a means towards progress. What man is able to destroy in pursuit of personal fulfillment is a marvel as well. To act as the adulteress woman mentioned, to sin and then continue on in life claiming to have done no wrong, can be too easy (30:20). Instead, we should be aware of and celebrate the importance of purity.

Agur Counts: the Size of Wise
Size is invariably equated with greatness. Agur, though, comments on the lessons that can be learned through observing some of the smaller inhabitants of earth. We should prepare for the future like the ants, create stability and security in our homes like the badgers, advance and improve

our positions in life like the locusts, and use our hands with skill like the spiders (30:25–28). By observing nature and applying what we see in the talents of even the smallest of God's creation, we can find wisdom.

In Our Homes
What Would You Wish for?
When Agur mentions the two things he requests before he dies, it makes me ponder the main desires of my heart. The things I've wanted most have changed throughout the years, as I've grown older (and hopefully wiser), and as my family has grown.

Families should be open to each other about their goals and dreams: meaning both the goals and dreams of the family unit and of the individual members. We should encourage each other along the path to fulfillment and talk about any wishes that might seem in opposition with the family's needs or God's will.

Jay has mentioned before that he wants to visit all of the major league baseball fields in America in his lifetime. During the first years of our marriage, I didn't pay any attention to this goal. I don't like baseball, and I didn't like the idea of revolving each family vacation around a different ballpark's location. After Jack's arrival, Jay mentioned how nice it would be if Jack could go to all the fields with him, how it would be something they could experience together as father and son. And then we started seeing how the ballparks were located by places I wanted to visit, with other entertainment offerings I enjoy. (Plus, I could always use a couple of hours in the hotel alone while the boys go to the game.)

This is not one of the major life goals Jay would mention if he were told to name only two, but this goal is doable, and it involves our family spending time together on new adventures. If our life objectives bring us closer to ourselves (personal development), our families (family development), or our career dreams (professional development)—all the while in harmony with our God (spiritual development)—then they are worth discussing, developing, and doing.

Empty No More
The empty tomb is a symbol of our ultimate fullness. The juxtaposition there is beautiful.

One of our challenges as Christians is to empty ourselves of the us-stuff and fill ourselves with the God-stuff. If we try to fill ourselves with world-stuff, we will always want more. If we look only to other people (even spouses or children or parents) to fill us, we will be disappointed.

We do have to be there for each other, and a home should never feel like rooms full of things and empty of love. But, at the center of every home, there must be the fullness of God. Let everything else be the detail work of this beautiful picture of wholeness.

Nature Knows
In the final two sections I wrote about (and in other parts of the chapter), Agur notices one of God's greatest object lessons—nature. My dad has always possessed a wonderment of nature; he uses his observations of God's creation as he teaches. My mom has always loved taking care of her yard. My brother and I grew up in the country, playing pretend in a wooded area we called Beaver Island (though my brother announced it was technically a peninsula since the creek didn't completely encircle the land).

I'm going to make a rather old-fashioned, out-dated, yet often-mentioned suggestion. Go outside. Yes, the weather isn't always perfect. I wrote part of this chapter outdoors in the depth of summer, and I was sweating before I could finish it. Yes, parts of nature are annoying such as bugs that bite or plants that itch or winds that blow your hair in your face. But there is so much beauty in the natural world. I am afraid we spend too much time enjoying the splendid achievements of man (which I am grateful for) and too little on the glorious achievements of God.

I didn't know there were a lot of nature references in this chapter when I sat to write on the back porch of a bed and breakfast in Gatlinburg, Tennessee, looking out over the mountains swelling in the distance and being distracted by a hummingbird and lizard who both kept approaching me. How much easier was it to write and reflect on the words of Agur, though, as I was surrounded by his descriptions (though thankfully no snakes were present).

God's creation can inspire us as it did Agur—in its magnitude or smallness, its strength or delicateness. We are part of this creation, and it's time we spent less time apart.

 hapter 31

Proverbs 31
The Words of King Lemuel's Mother
¹ The words of King Lemuel,
  the utterance which his
  mother taught him:
² What, my son?
  And what, son of my womb?
  And what, son of my vows?
³ Do not give your strength to women,
  Nor your ways to that which destroys kings.
⁴ It is not for kings, O Lemuel,
  It is not for kings to drink wine,
  Nor for princes intoxicating drink;
⁵ Lest they drink and forget the law,
  And pervert the justice of all the afflicted.
⁶ Give strong drink to him who is perishing,
  And wine to those who are bitter of heart.
⁷ Let him drink and forget his poverty,
  And remember his misery no more.
⁸ Open your mouth for the speechless,
  In the cause of all who are appointed to die.
⁹ Open your mouth, judge righteously,
  And plead the cause of the poor and needy.

The Virtuous Wife
¹⁰ Who can find a virtuous wife?
  For her worth is far above rubies.
¹¹ The heart of her husband safely trusts her;
  So he will have no lack of gain.
¹² She does him good and not evil
  All the days of her life.
¹³ She seeks wool and flax,
  And willingly works with her hands.
¹⁴ She is like the merchant ships,
  She brings her food from afar.
¹⁵ She also rises while it is yet night,
  And provides food for her household,
  And a portion for her maidservants.
¹⁶ She considers a field and buys it;
  From her profits she plants a vineyard.
¹⁷ She girds herself with strength,

And strengthens her arms.
¹⁸ She perceives that her merchandise is good,
And her lamp does not go out by night.
¹⁹ She stretches out her hands to the distaff,
And her hand holds the spindle.
²⁰ She extends her hand to the poor,
Yes, she reaches out her hands to the needy.
²¹ She is not afraid of snow for her household,
For all her household is clothed with scarlet.
²² She makes tapestry for herself;
Her clothing is fine linen and purple.
²³ Her husband is known in the gates,
When he sits among the elders of the land.
²⁴ She makes linen garments and sells them,
And supplies sashes for the merchants.
²⁵ Strength and honor are her clothing;
She shall rejoice in time to come.
²⁶ She opens her mouth with wisdom,
And on her tongue is the law of kindness.
²⁷ She watches over the ways of her household,
And does not eat the bread of idleness.
²⁸ Her children rise up and call her blessed;
Her husband also, and he praises her:
²⁹ " Many daughters have done well,
But you excel them all."
³⁰ Charm is deceitful and beauty is passing,
But a woman who fears the LORD,
she shall be praised.
³¹ Give her of the fruit of her hands,
And let her own works praise her in the gates.

In the Chapter
The Virtuous Wife: Clothing
"Who can find a virtuous wife?" Proverbs 31:10 begins. I appreciate that this chapter is said to be the words of Lemuel, who is sharing the teachings of his mother. She obviously wanted Lemuel to marry well, as she taught him a list of important characteristics for the ideal wife, whose "worth is far above rubies" (31:10).

The first descriptions I want to focus on deal with clothing, both literal and figurative. The term to be "girded" should bring the visual image of being surrounded, like a belt or girdle, that holds together tightly. She is surrounded and held together by her strength and honor and works hard to keep herself strong (31:17, 25). She takes care of her family's needs while still taking care of herself (31:21–22).

The Virtuous Wife: Planning, Preparing, and Processing
The virtuous wife is thoughtful and puts plans into action. Her husband can fully trust her to help him prosper and, perhaps the hardest verse for women to implement, always be good to him (31:11–12). This statement would imply that she never makes fun of or damages her husband's character in public, but instead praises him, which could be why her husband would be well known around important people (31:23).

She knows how to shop, work with her hands, and make sure her family is fed (31:13–15). But this women isn't talented at only housework; she is also a shrewd businesswoman, wise in the ways of investments (31:16, 18).

The Virtuous Wife: Praised
Not only is this woman concerned with the needs of her family, she is also mindful of others in need (31:20). Speaking in wisdom and kindness, she has a true reverence for her Father (31:26, 30). A woman with all of these characteristics deserves praise, from her children and her husband, who tell her she is the absolute best (31:28–31). Though two qualities prized by the world, it is not for her beauty (which declines) or charm (which deceives) that the virtuous wife gains this acclaim, but for her hard work, wisdom, and respect (31:30–31).

In Our Homes

A couple of questions arise from Proverbs 31. 1) Isn't this a tall order for one woman to fill? 2) Where is the chapter on the virtuous husband?

Have no fear: I can answer both questions. 1) Yes. 2) It's here too.

The First Question
First of all, yes, this is a tall order. As a wife, I want to protest. As a mother of a son, with another on the way, I want to cheer. I want to tell Jack

and Jonas that this is exactly the kind of woman they should be looking for. So, then, shouldn't I be this woman for my own husband?

Convicted? I am.

But my sons are a perfect little blessing, and my husband is…well…good, but….I guess I shouldn't double-standard the men in my house. Besides, words aren't nearly as powerful as actions. If I want my boys to see the value of waiting for this kind of woman, my best bet is to model just how priceless such a wife can be. If I am ever blessed with a daughter, she needs to see the flourish of a home whose heart is run by such a woman, so that she desires to develop these attributes as well, becoming a virtuous lady herself.

The Second Question
Some women may feel a little singled out in this chapter. Why are we given a guideline for how to behave? Well, for one, how nice that we are! How nice to know what is expected of me. We may not be able to fit the mold of the seemingly perfect mothers and wives we see set before us in our lives; perhaps our mashed potatoes come out gloopy or our sewing skills make a patch up job obvious. But we can look to the heart of Proverbs 31 and see how to righteously run our households: through hard work, planning, kindness, wisdom, respect, and praise (both to and from our husbands and children).

And this list is pointed to men as well. Not only is it a guide to encourage men to marry a good woman, it is a reminder to notice that good woman throughout your marriage. What does she bring you? Security, honor, and comfort. These blessings can become part of the routine for a man, and he can forget to acknowledge their worth.

So men, Proverbs 31 charges you—as an example to your sons to do the same, as an example to your daughters to see the value of their true worth, and as a well-deserved gesture of your gratitude to your wife—to praise the woman doing it all, for all of you.

A Spouseless House

And if you are running a one-parent household, Proverbs 31 is not null-and-void. For fathers without wives, please find a virtuous woman (an aunt, grandmother, cousin, babysitter, teacher, or friend) who can shine as an example for your children. For mothers without husbands, the attributes set forth in this chapter are still a valid route to virtuousness, though some of the wording will change ("wife" to "woman," for example) as you apply it to your lives.

References

"Countenance." *Dictionary.com*. n.p. n.d. Web. 26 July 2011.

Shakespeare, William. "Quotation Details." *The Quotations Page*. n.p. n.d. Web. 20 July 2011.

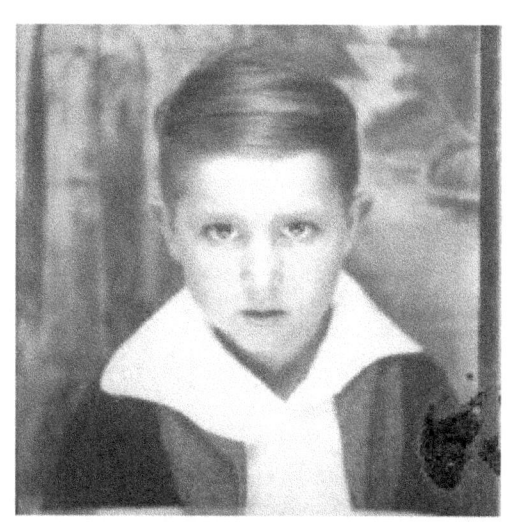

About the Authors

Jack Hilliard

Jack Hilliard is a native of West Tennessee. He received his Bachelor's degree from Freed-Hardeman University in Henderson, Tennessee, and his Master's degree in Counseling and Guidance from the University of Memphis in Memphis, Tennessee. He has spent his entire life as a preacher for Churches of Christ: preaching, teaching, and studying all over the world. He has traveled to eleven countries and driven, literally, from coast to coast within the United States. One trip to the Bible Lands gave Jack the opportunity to share a series of Bible Land Lectures on his experience.

Mr. Hilliard has lived most of his life in church service in the southern parts of the United States including Kentucky, Missouri, and Tennessee. Much of this life vocation took place in mission fields including Bermuda and the Appalachian Mountains. For the last four decades he has lived with his wife of sixty years, Lola Carter Hilliard, in Henderson, Tennessee, where they both retired from Freed-Hardeman University. In addition to preaching and university administration, Jack has taught on the radio for fourteen years, written regular newspaper articles for over seventeen years, and made several appearances on live television. He has counseled on marriage, finance, spirituality, and a variety of behavior health issues including mental, emotional, and physical health.

While preaching, sometimes part-time and other times full-time, Jack also worked in a variety of other professions including sales and public relations—for an insurance company and two colleges. He also owned two businesses. In his early career Jack served as president and vice president of multiple civic clubs, was the president of three PTA organizations, was a member of the board of trustees for three children's homes, and served as the chairman of the Jellico, Tennessee, Area Health Council. Jack worked for eighteen years with Freed-Hardeman University: in admissions, as Director of Placement, and as Director of Church Relations. His wife, Lola, worked many of those years by his side. The couple retired from full-time employment in 1994. Since retirement Hilliard has been busy with mission work, teaching, traveling, and writing. This is his ninth book.

Jack and Lola Hilliard have three children, four grandchildren, and five great grandchildren. In addition to their multiple responsibilities during retirement, they both love to spend time, as often as possible, with their family.

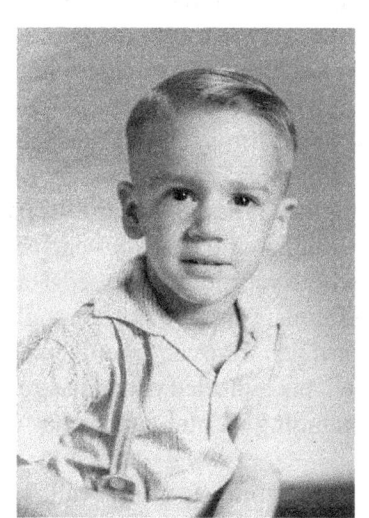

K. Mark Hilliard

Dr. Mark Hilliard received his bachelor's degree from Freed-Hardeman University in Community Health; his M.S. from Middle Tennessee State University in Community, School, and Public Health and Wellness Education; and his Doctor of Arts Degree from Middle Tennessee State University with major study in Human Performance, Behavioral Science, and Physical Education. He completed his dissertation and has conducted extensive research into the unique learning styles of Native Americans, specifically the Eastern Band of the Cherokee, and he oversees a yearly cultural study course on the Cherokee Reservation, conducts wellness education workshops on the Reservation, and is a minister for a Cherokee Missions Church on the Reservation in Cherokee, North Carolina.
Dr. Hilliard recently retired from O'More College of Design where he served for fourteen years as the President and CEO. Previous to that appointment, he served as the Provost, Executive Vice President, Academic Dean, and as a Full-Professor of Behavioral Science. He also taught adjunct courses at Middle Tennessee State University and Columbia State Community College, served as the medical director of the Tennessee Division of the American Cancer Society, and was a wildlife biologist with the U.S. Department of the Interior, Young Adult Conservation Corp. He is a Visiting Fellow and member of the Summer Research Institute at Harris Manchester College, Oxford University, and a former member of The Oxford Roundtable. A published author of three books on wellness, spirituality, and sensory education and experience, Professor Hilliard is working on his forth book, Sacred Places—Sacred Spaces.
He and his wife of thirty-seven years currently reside in Franklin, Tennessee. They have two grown children of their own, both educators, and four grandchildren–future educators.

Jessa Hilliard Sexton

In kindergarten, Jessa knew she wanted to be a teacher. Basing her early decision on a desire to write on the chalkboard whenever she pleased, Sexton has now developed a more sophisticated educational drive. At Harding University, she received a bachelor of arts in English with teacher licensure and a Masters of Education with an emphasis in English.

She was first published in her elementary school's literary magazine for a rather repetitive poem she wrote about lightning in the 4th grade. The writing bug has had a grip on her immune system ever since. Once through O'More Publishing and now printed with Hilliard Press, her children's books, textbooks, devotionals, and educational guides reflect her love of research, writing, and ever-learning.

Professor Sexton taught and tutored for nine years on writing, literature, education, research, and speech to ninth grade through college level including positions as graduate assistant in the Harding University Writing Lab, teacher at Searcy High School and with Upward Bound (the latter being a government-funded educational resource for low-income or possible first-generation college students), and Associate Professor at O'More College of Design.

Sexton lives in Franklin, Tennessee, with her husband of eight years and their two-year-old son, Jack. She was expecting her second son during the writing of this book, and Jonas is now six months old at the book's publication. Her favorite pastimes include reading books and singing to her sons, creating music with her husband, watching British television, shopping online or on the clearance racks, playing Mah jongg or going out to eat with friends, and writing and reading whenever she gets a chance.

# Other Books by the Authors

Jack Hilliard

Other books by this author deal with heritage, family, faith, and other inspiring and life-affecting topics:

My Mother Built the Fire
The Fire Still Burns
The Cadillac Years
Somewhere Beyond Yesterday
Beyond Today
After Tomorrow
Pain and Suffering: Friend or Foe?

K. Mark Hilliard

The Catcher of Dreams
Spirit-Ritual
Educational Wellness (co-written with Jessa Hilliard Sexton)
Sacred Spaces (to be published in 2012)

Jessa R. Sexton

Saturday illustrated by Jayne Williams
Educational Wellness (co-written with K. Mark Hilliard)
Hear and be Heard
Rose-Pie illustrated by Anastasia Morozova

hilliardpress.blogspot.com

www.ingramcontent.com/pod-product-compliance
Lightning Source LLC
LaVergne TN
LVHW061217060426
835508LV00014B/1335